CITE-CHECKER

The West Legal Studies Series

Administrative Law
Alternative Dispute Resolution
Bankruptcy
Business Organizations/Corporations
Civil Litigation and Procedure
CLA Exam Preparation
Client Accounting
Computer in the Law Office
Constitutional Law
Contract Law
Criminal Law and Procedure
Document Preparation
Environmental Law
Ethics

Family Law
Federal Taxation
Intellectual Property
Introduction to Law
Introduction to Paralegalism
Law Office Management
Law Office Procedures
Legal Research, Writing, and Analysis
Legal Terminology
Paralegal Employment
Real Estate Law
Reference Materials
Torts and Personal Injury Law
Will, Trusts, and Estate Administration

You will find unparalleled, practical support

Each book is augmented by instructor and student supplements to ensure the best learning experience possible. We also offer custom publishing and other benefits such as West's Student Achievement Award. In addition, our sales representatives are ready to provide you with dependable service.

We want to hear from you

Our best contributions for improving the quality of our books and instructional materials is feedback from the people who use them. If you have a question, concern, or observation about any of our materials, or you have a product proposal or manuscript, we want to hear from you. Please contact your local representative or write us at the following address:

West Legal Studies, 3 Columbia Circle, P.O. Box 15015, Albany, NY 12212-5015

For additional information point your browser at
www.westlegalstudies.com

CITE-CHECKER

A Hands-On Guide
to Learning Citation Form

Deborah E. Bouchoux
Georgetown University

Australia Canada Mexico Singapore Spain United Kingdom United States

WEST LEGAL STUDIES

Cite-Checker
by Deborah E. Bouchoux

Business Unit Director:
Susan L. Simpfenderfer

Editorial Assistant:
Lisa Flatley

Executive Production Manager:
Wendy A. Troeger

Executive Editor:
Marlene McHugh Pratt

Executive Marketing Manager:
Donna J. Lewis

Production Editor:
Betty L. Dickson

Acquisitions Editor:
Joan M. Gill

Channel Manager:
Wendy Mapstone

Cover Design:
Dutton and Sherman Design

Printed in Canada
1 2 3 4 5 XXX 05 04 03 02 01 00

For more information, contact Delmar,
3 Columbia Circle, PO Box 15015, Albany, NY 12212-5015.
Or find us on the World Wide Web at
http://www.westlegalstudies.com

For permission to use material from this text or product, contact us by
Tel   (800) 730-2214
Fax   (800) 730-2215
www.thomsonrights.com

Library of Congress Cataloging-in-Publication Data

Bouchoux, Deborah E., 1950–
  Cite-Checker / Deborah E. Bouchoux
  p. cm.
  Includes index
  ISBN 0-7668-1893-4
  1. Citation of Legal authorities--United States. I. Title.

KF245 .B68 2000
340'.01'48--dc21   00-043444

NOTICE TO THE READER

Dedication

For my husband, Donald, and our children
Meaghan, Elizabeth, Patrick, and Robert

Contents

Preface

INTRODUCTION

The task of checking one's own citations or those of another author to ensure they comply with the format of *The Bluebook: A Uniform System of Citation* (Columbia Law Review Ass'n et al. eds., 17th ed. 2000) is usually called cite-checking or "Bluebooking." The *Bluebook* consists of more than 300 pages of rules. Some of these rules are poorly explained while others are inconsistent and arbitrary. For example, when sending a reader to a page within an immediately preceding authority, one uses the form "*id.* at 16." However, when sending the reader to a paragraph or section within an immediately preceding authority, one uses "*id.* § 16" or "*id.* ¶ 16." In other words, one cannot use the word "at" before a section symbol or paragraph sign. Why? No one knows. Similarly, one must place a comma after the title of a law review article or annotation but not after a book title. These and myriad other inconsistencies make cite-checking a frustrating task for nearly all legal writers.

For practitioners, the task is complicated even further by the fact that the *Bluebook* is designed for use by law students. Most of the examples given in the *Bluebook* are presented in a particular style of typeface, called "large and small capitals," that practitioners seldom, if ever, use. Moreover, case names throughout nearly all of the *Bluebook* are neither underscored nor italicized while practitioners always underscore or italicize case names.

In sum, practitioners have lacked a clear and brief guide to citation form designed exclusively for them. After years of teaching legal research and providing numerous in-house seminars for practitioners at law firms, government agencies, and in-house legal departments, it became clear to me that practitioners were woefully underserved by the *Bluebook*. It is the author's hope that this book fills the need for a short and simple guide to the most common types of citations used by practitioners so that the task of cite-checking will be easier and less frustrating.

USE OF THIS BOOK

All legal authorities can be categorized into one of two broad categories: primary authorities and secondary authorities. Primary authorities include cases, statutes, constitutions, and administrative regulations (such as regulations of the FDA or FCC). Everything else (including books, articles, and law dictionaries) is a secondary authority. Legal writers typically prefer to cite primary authorities rather than secondary authorities because courts are bound to follow primary authorities from their jurisdiction, assuming these authorities are relevant or "on point." Primary authorities are thus usually referred to as "binding" or "mandatory," while secondary authorities are described as "persuasive."

This book is arranged in a "building block" approach. First, users should master primary authorities, namely, the most frequently cited authorities, cases, and statutes. They will then be ready to move on to secondary authorities and then to the use of quotations, signals, and short forms. In each instance, the *Bluebook* rules are explained and then examples (most of which are fictitious) are given.

For the most thorough mastery of citation form, users should start at Chapter 1 and continue reading through the text, doing the pertinent exercises along the way. Answer keys for each exercise are printed at the back of this book. While users will quickly be able to memorize some citation forms, most legal writers continually refer to the *Bluebook* to ensure a citation is correct. No one expects legal writers to have mastered all of the *Bluebook* rules together with their numerous exceptions. Thus, continual reference to the *Bluebook* while preparing answers to the exercises herein and while on the job is expected.

As new topics are introduced throughout this book, references will be given to the guiding rules or sections in the *Bluebook*. Thus, a reference to "Rule 15" refers to Rule 15 in the *Bluebook*, while a reference to "P.1" refers to Practitioners' Note 1 of the *Bluebook*. References to tables, such as Table T.1, refer to tables in the *Bluebook*.

When dates in sample citations are shown as "(19xx)," acceptable formats would include dates from other centuries if appropriate.

SCOPE OF THIS BOOK

This guide covers most of the basic citation rules, giving several examples. It is impossible, however, to give complete coverage to *Bluebook* rules without nearly duplicating the size of the original *Bluebook*. Moreover, there are authorities that even the *Bluebook* does not address. When confronted with such material, the *Bluebook* suggests that one try to locate an analogous authority, always being guided by the principle that a writer must ensure a reader can find the cited authority quickly and reliably.

While putting citations into their proper form is the hardest component of cite-checking, there is one other component to the task: "Shepardizing" (making sure authorities cited are still good law). This book does not cover Shepardizing. It is designed solely for the purpose of assisting legal writers in proper citation form. For information on Shepardizing (which is now done electronically rather than manually in most large law firms and departments), consult textbooks on legal research or access Shepard's website at <http://www.shepards.com> and use the tutorial to learn how to Shepardize.

Please note the Internet resources are of a time sensitive nature and URL addresses may often change or be deleted.

Contact us at westlegalstudies@delmar.com

Acknowledgments

No publication is the product solely of its author. Many individuals contributed significantly to the development of this guide to citation form. As always, my first thoughts and gratitude go to Susan M. Sullivan, Program Director of the Lawyer's Assistant Program at the University of San Diego, who provided me with my first teaching opportunity. Sue is a valued colleague and a dear friend.

My present program director, Gloria Silvers of the Legal Assistant Program at Georgetown University in Washington, DC, has been of invaluable assistance and encouragement to me.

Special thanks to my many students who, with their probing questions and curiosity, prompted me to continue trying to master the intricacies of the *Bluebook*. The reviewers who evaluated the manuscript of this publication provided prompt and clear analysis and must, therefore, be recognized:

Ms. Suzanne Bailey, Western Illinois University
Mr. Adam Epstein, University of Tennessee
Mr. John Frank, Chippewa Valley Technical College
Mr. Chris Whaley, Roane State Community College
Ms. Donna Bookin, Mercy College
Ms. Julia O. Tryk, Cuyahoga Community College
Ms. Patricia Adongo, University of LaVerne
Ms. Barbara Ricker, Andover College

I would like to express my most sincere appreciation to the following individuals at West Legal Studies who provided continued encouragement and support throughout the development of *Cite-Checker*: Joan Gill, Acquisitions Editor; Lisa Flatley, Editorial Assistant; and Betty Dickson, Production Editor.

Finally, deepest thanks and love to my husband Don and our children Meaghan, Elizabeth, Patrick, and Robert, for their unflagging patience and understanding while I continually pored over the *Bluebook* while writing this guide to citation form.

I would also like to thank West Group for its permission to reprint Figure 3–4, the map of the thirteen federal judicial circuits that appears in Chapter 3.

CHAPTER 1 Introduction to Cite-Checking

THE TASK OF CITE-CHECKING

A 300-plus page book entitled *The Bluebook: A Uniform System of Citation* (Columbia Law Review Ass'n et al. eds., 17th ed. 2000) (the *Bluebook*) is the standard reference tool in the United States for citing legal authorities. Although some states, including California and Michigan, have their own citation systems and some courts have established rules governing citation for documents submitted to them, the *Bluebook* remains the gold standard for citation form.

The principle underlying the *Bluebook* is that citation form for cases, statutes, and other authorities should be consistent throughout the entire United States, so that a practitioner in Ohio can submit a brief to a New York court and all readers will know how and where to locate the authorities referred to in the document. The task of placing citations in their proper format is typically called "cite-checking" or "Bluebooking."

Why must a practitioner learn the intricate and difficult rules of citation form? First, citation form communicates critical information to a reader because it allows a reader to locate and review authorities referred to in a legal document. Thus, an organized, systematic, uniform system of citation is needed so all law practitioners cite cases, statutes, and other authorities the same way each time they are used. Second, while incorrect citation form is not an act of legal malpractice, it reflects badly on you and your firm or company, much the same way a spelling error has a disproportionately negative effect on a reader. Carelessness in citation form may lead a reader to believe you are equally careless in your analysis of the law. Law firms and departments strive for excellence and professionalism to best serve their clients. Correct citation form is an integral part of this goal. Nevertheless, there is tremendous inconsistency in citation form often contributed to by

1

courts themselves, which frequently use incorrect citation form in their own published opinions. Similarly, law book publishers contribute to misunderstanding of citation form by often using incorrect citation form.

THE *BLUEBOOK*

Introduction

The *Bluebook* is the accepted "bible" for citation form (unless court rules dictate otherwise). Yet its myriad rules are awkwardly phrased, haphazardly arranged, and seemingly contradictory. Why? The *Bluebook* was originally intended as a short guide to aid law students in preparing citations in their scholarly writings. Eventually, as legal authorities proliferated, so did the rules in the *Bluebook*. Additionally, it began to be accepted as the citation form authority for practitioners as well as for those engaged in scholarly writing, although the presentation style used for scholarly writing (a style that used LARGE AND SMALL CAPITALS) could not be reproduced by practitioners who were typing their documents rather than having them professionally typeset. Thus, one citation guide attempts to fit vastly differing needs.

Moreover, the *Bluebook*'s coverage may simply be too broad. In providing information about citing to Swiss civil law cases, the East African Court of Appeals, and the Tasmanian Statutory Rules, little space is available to provide examples of far less esoteric citation forms, such as those for New York cases.

Thus, the *Bluebook*'s numerous rules and their exceptions, dual approach, and broad coverage have contributed to frustration for cite-checkers. Moreover, the task of cite-checking is often done at the eleventh hour, making it difficult and pressure-filled. Finally, it requires attention to detail and a high level of concentration to locate minute errors in spacing and abbreviations. All of these factors contribute to an often difficult task. By learning the most frequently used citation rules, however, in a step-by-step approach, you will achieve mastery of this task.

While there are other citation guides, such as *The Maroon Book* (published by Northwestern University and used primarily in the Chicago metropolitan area), the *Bluebook* is the most widely adopted system of citation and should be followed unless court rules or law firm or company policy require otherwise.

History of the *Bluebook*

The *Bluebook* is compiled by the editors of the *Columbia Law Review, Harvard Law Review, University of Pennsylvania Law Review,* and the *Yale Law Journal.* Originally compiled in the mid-1920s, the *Bluebook* was a small pamphlet designed to instruct scholarly writers and the printers of scholarly articles in citation form. Over the years, the *Bluebook* was revised a number of times. The present edition in use is the Seventeenth Edition. Earlier editions have little, if any, practical value and can be discarded. New editions are not released at regularly scheduled intervals but rather when the editors believe changes are needed. The Seventeenth Edition was issued in late 2000 and includes changes dictated by new technologies (such as instructions on citing to the Internet, e-mail correspondence, and CD-ROM).

Changes in the *Bluebook* over time may result in some citations being incorrect now that may have been correct several years ago when they were first prepared. Thus, exercise care when importing citations from a previously written document into your document. Ensure citations you use conform to present-day *Bluebook* rules.

Organization of the *Bluebook*

Spend a few minutes becoming familiar with the organization of the *Bluebook.* In particular, note the following:

* Examine the Preface to the Seventeenth Edition (page v). This page outlines changes made in the Seventeenth Edition of the *Bluebook.* When the next edition of the *Bluebook* is issued, examine this page to learn new rules and changes.

* Review the section on light blue paper beginning on page 10, called Practitioners' Notes. The examples found on pages 11–19 are ready for use by practitioners, meaning there is no need to convert typeface or make other changes to adapt *Bluebook* forms, originally intended for scholarly writers, for use in the "real world."

* Note Table T.1. After setting forth rules about federal court cases, there is a section devoted to citation form for the states, each of which is listed in alphabetical order. A reference is provided for each state's judicial website. While you will not be given many examples, you will be provided with a blueprint for setting up citations for the cases and statutes in each state.

- Table T.11 provides abbreviations for each state. Note that the abbreviations may not conform to your expectation as to how to abbreviate a particular state's name. Similarly, Table T.13 provides abbreviations for the months of the year. These are but two examples of the *Bluebook*'s insistence on uniformity.

- The Index, printed on white paper at the end of the *Bluebook* provides a ready reference to locating information. It is well-organized and complete.

TOP TEN TIPS FOR EFFECTIVE CITE-CHECKING

Because cite-checking is typically an eleventh-hour assignment and requires painstaking attention to detail, the task requires patience and a highly organized approach. The following tips will make your task more manageable.

1. **Highlight all citations.** Your first step should be to take a colored marker and highlight all citations (both primary and secondary authorities) in a document. You may be surprised to discover that after an hour or so, the citations tend to blend into the text of the document, particularly when italics are used rather than underscoring. Thus, if you highlight each citation when you are fresh, you will readily be able to locate and check each citaton when your attention may be flagging.

2. **Get instructions.** If cite-checking for another, ask the author or the supervisor who assigned the cite-checking assignment whether you can assume numbers and dates are correct and that you, therefore, need only check spacing, punctuation, and other format considerations or whether you should do a "top to bottom" check and verify the accuracy of every number and date. When in doubt, err on the side of caution and do the most thorough check possible. Similarly, ask if the author or the judge to whom the document is being sent has a preference for underscoring rather than italicizing case names and book titles. This will save time later if your first draft uses italics and the author or judge insists all case names and book titles be underscored.

3. **Ask for help.** If cite-checking for another writer, call or e-mail your colleagues and ask if anyone has done a cite-checking assignment

for the particular author and whether the author has any particular preferences or quirks. Similarly, if the document is addressed to a court, ask if anyone has recently filed a document with that court. Using a model will give you a certain comfort level. Save your cite-checked briefs and make your own model form files.

4. **Know the rules.** Some courts have mandated their own rules for citation form. If your document is addressed to a court, determine if such rules exist. If they do, they supersede the *Bluebook* rules. To determine whether court rules exist, ask your law librarian (if your firm has one) to call the clerk of the court and inquire, or check the Internet. For home pages of the federal appellate courts, access http://www.law.emory.edu/FEDCTS/ and follow the instructions to locate rules of court for each circuit and the Supreme Court. For state court rules, access http://www.ll.georgetown.edu and follow the instructions to obtain information about "state, local, & territorial law." When you are presented with a map of the United States, point and click on your state. You will then be provided with a section on the judiciary of your state, which usually includes court rules. Check Table T.1 of the *Bluebook*, which identifies judicial websites for each state. Similarly, some law firms and law departments have their own practices and procedures for citation form. Ask if such policies exist.

5. **Support your corrections.** As you correct citations in the document, write legibly so the individual who later word processes the document can readily make the appropriate corrections. Note on your draft the page of the *Bluebook* or the pertinent rule that supports your correction. For example, if the author has used a broken line for the signal <u>cert. denied</u> and your review of page 12 of the *Bluebook* shows it as <u>cert. denied</u>, jot "page 12" near your correction. If the author later challenges your correction, you will be prepared to show support for your work. What should you do if an author ignores your correct work and insists on using an incorrect form? Give in. The person who signs the document should have the final decision on its contents.

6. **Develop a system.** As you make corrections, use a code or system to remind yourself which citations have been checked and which remain to be corrected. Use checks, asterisks, colored pens, colored adhesive flags, or any other method that works for you. Then if your

work is interrupted and you later need to return to the project, you can readily determine where you need to start.

7. **Work smart.** As you correct citations, you will undoubtedly notice that there are "holes" in the document, such as missing dates or missing pages of quotes. Rather than immediately filling in each gap as you come across it, mark each gap with a colored highlighter or adhesive flag. Later, you can either go to the law library or go on-line and locate all of the missing information in one efficient step rather than attempting a piecemeal approach.

8. **Be thorough.** Check all citations in the document. Ignore the temptation to focus on the argument section of a brief. Start at page one and look for every citation in the document, including those in the table of authorities, in footnotes, and any citations in any appendices.

9. **Be consistent.** If the author has been underscoring case names, ensure that book titles and citation signals such as <u>id.</u> and <u>supra</u> are likewise underscored. Conversely, if case names have been italicized, italicize book titles and signals.

10. **Check the signals.** Citation signals such as *id.* tell a reader that a previously given citation supports a later statement. If you see signals such as *id.* and *supra,* check to ensure they match up with a previous citation. Why would they not? On many occasions an author may omit, insert, or move a section of a brief, forgetting that following signals may then be left hanging without a previous reference.

CHAPTER 2 The *Bluebook* Trap: Typeface Conventions

Guiding Principle: Practitioners should be wary of most of the examples given in the Bluebook *other than those in Section P, entitled Practitioners' Notes. While the words in the examples are in the right order, the presentation style is inappropriate for practitioners in that large and small capitals are used. According to the* Bluebook, *practitioners cannot use large and small capitals and must convert any large and small capital styles to ordinary roman typeface.*

THE PROBLEM

Examine the inside front cover of the *Bluebook*, left-hand side, approximately halfway down the page. Note the reference to the following state constitution:

N.M. Const. art. IV, § 7.

Now examine the inside back cover of the *Bluebook* in the same location. Examine the reference to the same constitution:

N.M. Const. art. IV, § 7.

Can you tell the difference in the style in which the same source is presented?

Note that in the first example, the capital letters "N," "M," and the "C" in "Const." are all slightly larger than the remaining capital letters in the word "Const." while in the second example on the inside back cover the presentation shows only an initial capital letter.

What is going on? How can both be correct? Return to your copy of the *Bluebook*. Note the heading on the inside front cover: Quick Reference: Law Review Footnotes. Compare this with the heading on the inside back cover: Quick Reference: Court Documents and Legal Memoranda.

You are now ready to tackle perhaps the single most confusing thing about the *Bluebook*. Nearly all of the examples given are for use in law review footnotes rather than for use by practitioners.

The *Bluebook* Approach

The *Bluebook* was developed solely for citations appearing in scholarly and academic articles appearing in law school publications, namely "law reviews." Only later was it adopted for general use by "practitioners," those people functioning in the "real world" of law practice. At the time the *Bluebook* was created, law review articles were generally typeset by professional printers who were able to use a format consisting of large and small capitals in which the first letter of a major word was displayed in a larger size capital letter than other letters in the word (for example, TRUSTS AND ESTATES).

Practitioners' Approach

Because practitioners used typewriters to prepare briefs and documents rather than having them typeset by printers, they could not reproduce the large and small capital presentation dictated by the *Bluebook,* and as a result, practitioners began converting the large and small capital formats shown in the *Bluebook* to a simpler style, generally referred to as "ordinary roman type" (for example, Trusts and Estates). Ordinary roman type is the typeface most often used in books, newspapers, and magazines. Popular roman styles include Times New Roman and Garamond.

A DUAL SYSTEM OF CITATION

A twofold citation system thus developed with law reviews showing citations for statutes, constitutions, books, and periodical names in large and small capitals and practitioners showing those same citations in the simpler form, because practitioners were incapable at that time of producing large and small capitals on standard office typewriters.

Unfortunately, the dual system is generally not explained well (or even at all) to law or paralegal students or to those word processors who prepare briefs and other documents for practitioners. Some law students exited law school believing citations should be displayed in large and small capital letters only to discover that they must learn to convert most of the examples found in the *Bluebook* in order to comport with the style used by practitioners.

You may wonder why the dual system persists when, with today's word processors, it is easily possible for practitioners to use the large and small capital format. Such would result in a truly "uniform" system of citation with both law students and real-world practitioners presenting all citations in the same style. There is no good answer to this question. The dual system has persisted long after any need for it compels its use.

There are some other differences in the manner in which citations are presented in law review footnotes and in practitioners' documents. For example, return to the inside front and back covers of the *Bluebook* and note that in law review footnotes, case names and book titles are not underscored while they are underscored by practitioners. Other differences will be discussed later. For now, it is enough for you to know that court documents and legal memoranda never use large and small capitals.

THE *BLUEBOOK'S* ADVICE (RULE 2; P.1)

The *Bluebook* itself makes only passing references to the confusing and seldom understood rule requiring differing presentation styles when one is preparing a law review article and when one is preparing a court document.

As discussed previously, the inside front and back covers of the *Bluebook* note that there is a difference in the typeface used in law review footnotes and that used by practitioners. Similarly, Rule 2 in the *Bluebook*, entitled Typefaces for Law Reviews, mentions the distinction; however, it merely instructs practitioners to assume the affirmative duty of substituting the typeface conventions found in the first section of the *Bluebook*, Practitioners' Notes (a mere nine pages), for those found in the remainder of the *Bluebook* (approximately 350 pages) and confirms that large and small capitals do not appear in court documents and legal memoranda. P.1(b) adds that practitioners do not use large and small capitals. Finally, P.1(h) provides a rather global instruction that practitioners should print reporters, constitutions, statutes, restatements, and a few other sources in ordinary roman type (rather than in *italics* or in LARGE AND SMALL CAPITALS). Thus, practitioners are primarily left to their own devices to figure out that most of the *Bluebook* is not for them. They will have to convert every instance of LARGE AND SMALL CAPITALS to a simpler style, namely ordinary roman type.

Lesson: If you are a practitioner, never use LARGE AND SMALL CAPITALS. In every instance in which you see such a presentation style in the Bluebook, *immediately convert it to the simpler style used by practitioners.*

If you have trouble remembering this rule, as you see examples throughout the *Bluebook,* ask yourself: Could I reproduce this presentation on an old-fashioned typewriter? If the answer is "no," it is a signal that the presentation was meant for printers who could manually typeset law review articles, not for practitioners.

Exercise for Chapter 2

The following are examples found in the *Bluebook.* Correct them for use by practitioners.

1.   RESTATEMENT (THIRD) OF UNFAIR COMPETITION § 3 (1985).

———————————————————————

2.   U.S. CONST. art. 1, § 9, cl. 2.

———————————————————————

3.   CAL. VEH. CODE § 11,509 (West 1987 & Supp. 1991).

———————————————————————

4.   17 AM. JUR. 2d *Contracts* § 74 (1964).

———————————————————————

5.   Kim Lane Scheppele, *Foreword: Telling Stories,* 87 MICH. L. REV. 2073, 2082 (1989).

———————————————————————

6.   S. REP. NO. 89–910, at 4 (1965).

———————————————————————

CHAPTER 3 Citation Form for Cases

INTRODUCTION

There are several important rules to know about cases, primarily rules dealing with case names, rules relating to citation form for state and federal court cases, and related rules about abbreviations and spacing in case citations.

The required elements of a case citation are as follows:

- The name of the case

- A reference to the published source(s) where the case can be located

- Parenthetical information consisting of the date of decision and an identification of the court that issued the decision (if such is not apparent from the name of the set itself)

- Subsequent history of the case (if any)

CASE NAMES (RULE 10.2)

The rules relating to case names are discussed in *Bluebook* Rule 10.2. Some of the more critical rules are as follows:

- Case names may be <u>underscored</u> or *italicized*. While the *Bluebook* states in P.1 that underscoring is more prevalent, this may not be true in your office. Moreover, some writers have a strong preference for one approach rather than another. It is possible that older practitioners who began careers before the advent of computers prefer underscoring because the typewriters on which they prepared their documents were not capable of any other style while younger practitioners may prefer italicizing because they are familiar with word processors that are capable of italicizing. Either approach is acceptable.

- When underscoring, underscore the entire case name using a solid unbroken line, including the "<u>v.</u>" (P.1(a)) and any procedural phrase such as "<u>In re</u>."

- The "v." in a case citation is always a lowercase letter followed by a period.

- If the case names ends with an abbreviated word such as "<u>Inc.</u>" or "<u>Corp.</u>," underscore or italicize the period in the abbreviation.

- Follow case names with a comma, which is neither underscored nor italicized.

- Give last names only of the parties in the case. Omit first names or initials, although always reproduce a business name scrupulously even if its name includes a person's name, as in *Carr v. Perry Ellis Co.*

- If there are multiple plaintiffs and defendants, list only the first plaintiff and the first defendant. Drop all other parties from the citation and do not indicate that there are multiple parties by using an expression such as "et al.," a phrase meaning "and others."

- Do not identify the status of a party by including a term such as "plaintiff," "trustee," or "executor."

- Generally omit prepositional phrases of location (thus, the citation *Brown v. Board of Education* is correct while *Brown v. Board of Education of Topeka, Kansas* is not).

- Criminal cases from your state will be titled *State v. Lee, People v. Lee,* or *Commonwealth v. Lee* (if the case originates in the commonwealth of Kentucky, Massachusetts, Pennsylvania, or Virginia). When the criminal case leaves your jurisdiction and goes to the U.S. Supreme Court on appeal, its name will change to *Arizona v. Lee* or *Pennsylvania v. Lee,* probably to facilitate indexing of case names.

- If the case name includes two business designations, such as both "Inc." and "Co.," retain the first and strike the second.

- Do not abbreviate "United States" in a case name.

- If one of the parties is commonly referred to in spoken language by its initials rather than its full name (FBI, CIA, SEC), you may use that abbreviation and not include any periods (thus, *NLRB* is correct while *N.L.R.B.* is not) (Rule 6.1(b)).

ABBREVIATIONS IN CASE NAMES (RULE 10.2.1(c); TABLE T.6)

You may have already noticed that many case names are lengthy. What words can you abbreviate in a citation to save space? The answer depends on how the citation is presented to the reader.

Note that Rule 10.2.1(c) states that when case names appear in a textual sentence, you may abbreviate only widely known acronyms (such as FBI and FCC) and the following eight well-known abbreviations: &, Ass'n, Bros., Co., Corp., Inc., Ltd., and No.

Now examine Table T.6 of the *Bluebook*, which tells you that you should always abbreviate any of the more than 160 words listed, including words such as "Liab.," "Distrib.," and "Hous." Such words are to be abbreviated even if they are the first or only word in a case name. How can these two statements possibly be reconciled?

Consider the way in which legal writers make arguments. Most commonly, they will make a statement about the law in a declaratory sentence ending with a period and then follow that statement with a citation. To avoid a rigid and rote approach, however, writers will often interweave citations into the middle of sentences. Which words can be abbreviated depends on which of these two styles is selected. The two governing rules are as follows:

- If your citation appears as part of a textual sentence (meaning that the citation is needed to make sense of the sentence), you should not distract your reader with odd-looking abbreviations. Thus, you may only abbreviate widely known acronyms (such as FBI and CIA) and the highly familiar eight words identified previously (such as "Inc." and "Co.").

- If, on the other hand, your citation stands alone as its own statement in support of (or in contradiction to) a previous declaratory sentence, unusual abbreviations will not distract the reader, and you must thus use any of the more than 160 words listed in Table T.6 (such as "Pub." and "Tech.").

Examples:

* Punitive damages are recoverable in fraud actions. *W. Util. & Transp. Co. v. Lakewood Ref. Inc.*, 450 U.S. 24, 27 (1990).

* Although punitive damages are recoverable for fraud, *Western Utility & Transportation Co. v. Lakewood Refining Inc.*, 450 U.S. 24, 27 (1990), those damages must bear a rational relationship to actual damages. *Peterson Indem. Co. v. Int'l Lab. Co.*, 451 U.S. 191, 199 (1992).

Practice Tips:

✓ Write across the top of Table T.6 of your *Bluebook* the note "For Stand-Alone Citations Only" to remind you that the listed abbreviations can only be used when your citation stands alone as its own sentence.

✓ Unless otherwise indicated in Table T.6, to pluralize an abbreviation just add an "s" to the abbreviation (before the period), such as changing "Hosp." to "Hosps."

✓ If one of the eight well-known words (such as Co. or Inc.) begins a party's name, it cannot be abbreviated.

STATE COURT CASES (RULE 10.3; P.3)

Background

To master citation form for state court cases, one must understand how cases are published. Cases are published either officially (meaning their publication is mandated by a statute) or unofficially (meaning they are published without such authority). Years ago, nearly all states mandated that their appellate court cases that advanced legal theory be published. The sets of books that collected these decisions were called *reports* and generally were indicated by a state abbreviation ("Minn." for cases from Minnesota, "Cal." for cases from California, and so forth).

Because what courts decide is a matter of public record and is not subject to copyright protection, anyone can copy cases that are already published, print the cases, and bind them, perhaps adding some editorial features. Such a set is *unofficial,* meaning its publication is not authorized by the state legislature but is rather the result of some independent act of a third party.

Such action was undertaken by two brothers named West in the late 1800s. They republished cases that had already been published officially, grouped them together in various geographical units, and began selling the sets to practitioners. West Group thus produces the *North Western Reporter,* which publishes cases from North Dakota, South Dakota, Nebraska, Minnesota, Iowa, Wisconsin, and Michigan. A Wisconsin case that appears in the *North Western Reporter* is the same as the Wisconsin case published in the official *Wisconsin Reports,* although certain editorial enhancements may vary from set to set. Thus, the case *Brown v. Whitney* might be located at 432 Wis. 2d 13 and at 209 N.W.2d 421. The two citations are called *parallel* citations.

West Group also produces other sets of books that arrange cases published in certain geographical units. (See Figure 3–1.)

After West created the seven geographical units, it decided that certain states produced so much case law they should have their own sets of books, and so it created the *California Reporter,* the *New York Supplement,* and *Illinois Decisions* (for cases from those states). Thus, for example, a newer California Supreme Court case will have three parallel citations: a reference to its publication in the official *California Reports,* a reference to its publication in the *Pacific Reporter,* and a reference to its publication in the *California Reporter.*

Some practitioners might prefer to buy the official *California Reports* while others might prefer to obtain access to cases from surrounding states by purchasing the *Pacific Reporter.*

Citation Form

For nearly 70 years, the *Bluebook* required that practitioners provide all parallel citations when citing state court cases, reasoning that the author could not possibly know what set of books the reader had in his or her law office or judge's chambers, and thus, authors should provide

Atlantic Reporter	Connecticut, Delaware, Maine, Maryland, New Hampshire, New Jersey, Pennsylvania, Rhode Island, Vermont, Washington, D.C.
North Eastern Reporter	Illinois, Indiana, Massachusetts, New York, Ohio
South Eastern Reporter	Georgia, North Carolina, South Carolina, Virginia, West Virginia
Southern Reporter	Alabama, Florida, Louisiana, Mississippi
North Western Reporter	Iowa, Michigan, Minnesota, Nebraska, North Dakota, South Dakota, Wisconsin
South Western Reporter	Arkansas, Kentucky, Missouri, Tennessee, Texas
Pacific Reporter	Alaska, Arizona, California, Colorado, Hawaii, Idaho, Kansas, Montana, Nevada, New Mexico, Oklahoma, Oregon, Utah, Washington, Wyoming

Figure 3–1   West's National Reporter System for State Court Cases

all citations to enable a reader to locate easily any cited case. Writers were required to give the official citation first, followed by a comma and the unofficial citation.

In 1991, this rule changed. Although not stated as clearly as it could be, the rule relating to citation form for state court cases is now as follows:

- If you are citing a state court case in a document directed to a state court in that state, give all parallel citations, listing the official citation first and the unofficial citation(s) second.

- In any other instance (a letter to a client, an internal office memorandum, or a document directed to some court not in that state or to a federal court, wherever located), give only the regional citation (with a parenthetical indication of the deciding court and year of decision). (See P.3 and Rule 10.4.)

Thus, if you are citing a Virginia case in a document sent to a court in Virginia, give all parallel citations. If you are citing the same case in any other document, give only the regional citation. You may wish to reinterpret this rule as meaning "be polite to your state court judges because you do not know what set of books they have in their chambers." As always, if local rules exist regarding citation form, they supersede the *Bluebook* rules.

How will you know which is the official citation that must be placed first and which is the unofficial citation that must be placed second? The official citation includes an abbreviation for the state (such as "Cal." or "Ga."), while the unofficial citation is generally a regional abbreviation (such as "A." for "Atlantic," "S.E." for South Eastern, and so forth). The courts of each state are listed in the *Bluebook* in Table T.1 from highest court to lowest court.

Although the state-by-state summary in Table T.1 provides instruction on citing state court cases, the information in Table T.1 is directed to citation form for law review footnotes. Practitioners should thus follow the format and examples given in the Practitioners' Notes section of the *Bluebook*, which shows that all parallel citations should be given (with official citations given before unofficial regional citations) when citing a state court case in a document submitted to a state court in that state.

Remember that cases from California, Illinois, and New York may have three parallel citations, and you must order the citation as outlined in the *Bluebook*.

Examples (unless court or local rules require otherwise):

- *Martinez v. Sanders,* 360 Wis. 2d 118, 314 N.W.2d 21 (1994). This form is used when citing this Wisconsin case in a document addressed to a Wisconsin state court.

- *Martinez v. Sanders,* 314 N.W.2d 21 (Wis. 1994). This form is used when citing the *Martinez* case in any instance other than when the document is presented to a state court in Wisconsin.

Note: Although Wisconsin has now adopted a public domain citation format, that citation format is only for cases decided after January 1, 2000. Public domain citations are discussed later in this chapter.

Parentheticals for State Court Cases (Rule 10.4(b))

Note the parenthetical given in the preceding second example. Without the indication of "Wis." in the parenthetical, the reader would have no idea which of the seven states in the *North Western Reporter* issued the decision. The reader must be given this critical piece of information.

If the parenthetical merely gives the abbreviation for the state (such as "Cal." or "Wis."), it is an indication that the case is from the highest court in that state. (Rule 10.4(b)). If the case was decided by a court other than the highest court, you must indicate such in the parenthetical, generally by providing the abbreviation "Ct. App." For example, the citation *State v. Bowie*, 429 P.2d 136 (Cal. Ct. App. 1991), indicates the case is from the intermediate appellate court in California while the citation *Franks v. Park*, 436 P.2d 102 (Cal. 1992), indicates the case was decided by the highest court in California, the California Supreme Court. Similarly, "(Kan. 1996)" indicates a 1996 decision of the Kansas Supreme Court, while "(Kan. Ct. App. 1996)" indicates a 1996 decision of the Kansas Court of Appeals. When the state is clear from the name of the official reporter set (as it is in "Cal." or "Kan."), it is not needed in a parenthetical (see the preceding first example). Do not indicate the department or district that decided a case unless that information is particularly relevant. Note that there is a space before the parenthetical is opened.

In a few states, including Arizona, Idaho, New Mexico, South Carolina, and Wisconsin, cases from the state supreme court and from the state court of appeals are published in one set. For example, *Idaho Reports* publishes decisions from the Idaho Supreme Court and from the Idaho Court of Appeals. Because the name of the set, *Idaho Reports*, does not tell which court decided the case, additional information is required in the parenthetical, when referring to appellate court cases, as follows: *Bell v. Hall*, 204 Idaho 14, 611 P.2d 84 (Ct. App. 1990). Note that no reference to "Idaho" is given in the parenthetical because the reader can easily tell which state decided the case.

Some states, such as Alabama and Tennessee, have separate courts of criminal appeals. Citations to those cases would be given as follows:

State v. Harris, 82 Tenn. Crim. App. 141, 203 S.W.2d 18 (1995).

or

State v. Harris, 203 S.W.2d 18 (Tenn. Crim. App. 1995).

Finally, some states (Maine, Montana, Nevada, New Hampshire, Rhode Island, South Dakota, Vermont, West Virginia, and Wyoming) have no intermediate appellate courts. In those states, all citations are to the state supreme court.

Discontinuation of Some Official Reports

Because West's unofficial reporters became so successful and many practitioners preferred the West reporters over their own official state reports, a number of states (generally the less populous ones) ceased publishing officially. For cases from these states, you will only be able to cite to the unofficial regional reporter (and then provide the appropriate parenthetical information). You will not be able to include an official citation because one does not exist after the date official publication ceased. For cases decided prior to the date official publication ceased, follow the normal citation rules for state court cases discussed previously.

How can one determine if a state has discontinued official publication? Table T.1 of the *Bluebook* provides the answer. For example, note that the entry for West Virginia on page 239 states that the *West Virginia Reports* covers cases from "1864–date" while page 241 indicates that the *Wyoming Reports* covers cases from "1870–1959." Such is an indication that West Virginia is still publishing officially while Wyoming ceased official publication in 1959. Thus, for any case decided in Wyoming after 1959, the citation form is as follows:

> *Wong v. Harris*, 590 P.2d 118 (Wyo. 1985). (Note: For cases from Wyoming prior to 1959, you may need to include both parallel citations, namely to Wyo. and to P. or P.2d.)

See the Appendix, Examples of State Cases and Statutes, for sample citations for all states and the District of Columbia. See Figure 3–2 for a table of discontinued official state court reports.

PUBLIC DOMAIN CITATIONS (RULES 10.3.1; 10.3.3; P.3)

Both the American Bar Association (ABA) and the American Association of Law Libraries (AALL) have recommended that courts adopt a public domain citation system to allow a citation system for cases that would be equally effective whether the cases are found in conventional print form or in electronic form. The system is also referred to as "vendor neutral" or "medium neutral," meaning that the citation will look the same whether the case is found in a printed book, in CD-ROM form, or on the Internet.

Rule 10.3.1, in discussing parallel citations for state court cases, states that if a state court decision is available through an official public domain citation, this citation must be given, and a citation to the relevant regional reporter (A., P., S.W., and so forth) must be provided as well. To assist readers, the regional citation is included because it is so well recognized. Thus, the public domain citation really only replaces the official citation because the regional citation continues to exist. The citation should include the case name, year of decision, the state's two character postal code (found in Table T.1), abbreviation of court issuing the decision (unless the court is the state's highest court), sequential number of the decision, paragraph number (when one refers to specif-

State	Year of Discontinuation	State	Year of Discontinuation
Alabama	1976	Minnesota	1977
Alaska	Never published cases officially	Mississippi	1966
Colorado	1980	Missouri	1956
Delaware	1966	North Dakota	1953
District of Columbia	Never published cases officially	Oklahoma	1953
Florida	1948	Rhode Island	1980
Indiana	1981	South Dakota	1976
Iowa	1968	Tennessee	1971
Kentucky	1951	Texas	1962
Louisiana	1972	Utah	1974
Maine	1965	Wyoming	1959

Figure 3–2   Table of Discontinued Official State Court Reports

ic material in the case), and the regional citation. If the decision is unpublished, place a capital "U" after the sequential number. Note that public domain formats are adopted for use after specified dates. (See Table T.1.) Citation form for cases before the effective date should follow the format described earlier for state court cases.

Example:

Wade v. Lee, 1997 ME 44, ¶ 15, 401 A.2d 909, 914.

At this time, Arizona, Colorado, Louisiana, Maine, Mississippi, Montana, New Mexico, North Dakota, Oklahoma, South Dakota, Utah, and Wisconsin have adopted public domain citation systems, and Arkansas, Florida, Georgia, and Tennessee are considering doing so. When citing to cases from these states, check state and local rules and the examples shown in Table T.1 of the *Bluebook.* In the absence of instruction, follow the *Bluebook.* Additional information on this topic is found in Chapter 6. The *Bluebook* itself states that information on jurisdictions adopting a public domain format since publication of the Seventeenth Edition can be found at http://www.legalbluebook.com.

FEDERAL COURT CASES (TABLE T.1)

Background

To understand how to cite cases from our federal courts, you must first have a basic understanding of our federal court structure. The trial courts in our federal system are called "district courts." They may handle a wide variety of cases, from bank robbery to free speech to copyright cases. There are more than 90 district courts in the United States. Each state has at least one district court, and if a state has a heavy caseload and/or comprises a significant geographic area, it may have more than one district court. Thus, New Jersey has one district court while California has four district courts. (See Figure 3–3, which identifies district courts and U.S. courts of appeals.)

Litigants who lose a case in the district court can appeal an adverse decision to our intermediate federal courts of appeals. The United States is divided into 13 areas, called "circuits," with various states being grouped into a circuit. Thus, New York, Connecticut, and Vermont are in the Second Circuit, and most western states are in the

State	District Court	Circuit
Alabama	M.D. Ala., N.D. Ala., S.D. Ala.	11th Cir.
Alaska	D. Alaska	9th Cir.
Arizona	D. Ariz.	9th Cir.
Arkansas	E.D. Ark., W.D. Ark.	8th Cir.
California	C.D. Cal., E.D. Cal., N.D. Cal., S.D. Cal.	9th Cir.
Colorado	D. Colo.	10th Cir.
Connecticut	D. Conn.	2d Cir.
Delaware	D. Del.	3d Cir.
District of Columbia	D.D.C.	D.C. Cir.
Florida	M.D. Fla., N.D. Fla., S.D. Fla.	11th Cir.
Georgia	M.D. Ga., N.D. Ga., S.D. Ga.	11th Cir.
Hawaii	D. Haw.	9th Cir.
Idaho	D. Idaho	9th Cir.
Illinois	C.D. Ill., N.D. Ill., S.D. Ill.	7th Cir.
Indiana	N.D. Ind., S.D. Ind.	7th Cir.
Iowa	N.D. Iowa, S.D. Iowa	8th Cir.
Kansas	D. Kan.	10th Cir.
Kentucky	E.D. Ky., W.D. Ky.	6th Cir.
Louisiana	E.D. La., M.D. La., W.D. La.	5th Cir.
Maine	D. Me.	1st Cir.
Maryland	D. Md.	4th Cir.
Massachusetts	D. Mass.	1st Cir.
Michigan	E.D. Mich., W.D. Mich.	6th Cir.
Minnesota	D. Minn.	8th Cir.
Mississippi	N.D. Miss., S.D. Miss.	5th Cir.
Missouri	E.D. Mo., W.D. Mo.	8th Cir.

Figure 3–3   District Courts and U.S. Courts of Appeal

State	District Court	Circuit	State	District Court	Circuit
Montana	D. Mont.	9th Cir.	South Carolina	D.S.C.	4th Cir.
Nebraska	D. Neb.	8th Cir.	South Dakota	D.S.D.	8th Cir.
Nevada	D. Nev.	9th Cir.	Tennessee	E.D. Tenn.	6th Cir.
New Hampshire	D.N.H.	1st Cir.		M.D. Tenn.	
New Jersey	D.N.J.	3d Cir.		W.D. Tenn.	
New Mexico	D.N.M.	10th Cir.	Texas	E.D. Tex.	5th Cir.
New York	E.D.N.Y.	2d Cir.		N.D. Tex.	
	N.D.N.Y.			S.D. Tex.	
	S.D.N.Y.			W.D. Tex.	
	W.D.N.Y.		Utah	D. Utah	10th Cir.
North Carolina	E.D.N.C.	4th Cir.	Vermont	D. Vt.	2d Cir.
	M.D.N.C.		Virginia	E.D. Va.	4th Cir.
	W.D.N.C.			W.D. Va.	
North Dakota	D.N.D.	8th Cir.	Washington	E.D. Wash.	9th Cir.
Ohio	N.D. Ohio	6th Cir.		W.D. Wash.	
	S.D. Ohio		West Virginia	N.D.W. Va.	4th Cir.
Oklahoma	E.D. Okla.	10th Cir.		S.D.W. Va.	
	N.D. Okla.		Wisconsin	E.D. Wis.	7th Cir.
	W.D. Okla.			W.D. Wis.	
Oregon	D. Or.	9th Cir.	Wyoming	D. Wyo.	10th Cir.
Pennsylvania	E.D. Pa.	3d Cir.	U.S. Court of Appeals for the Federal Circuit	Fed. Cir.	
	M.D. Pa.				
	W.D. Pa.				
Rhode Island	D.R.I.	1st Cir.			

Figure 3–3   District Courts and U.S. Courts of Appeal (continued)

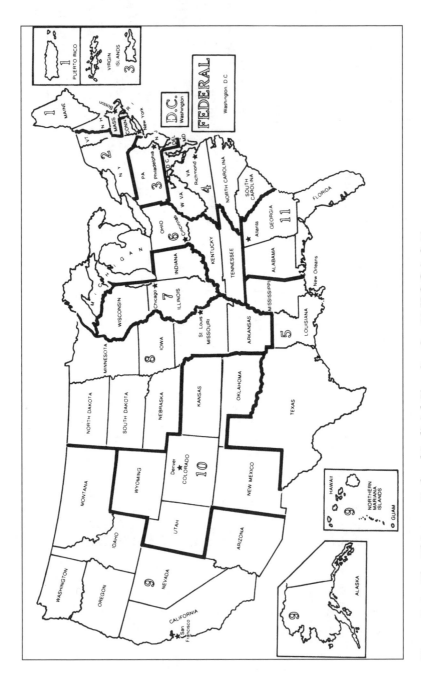

Figure 3–4   The Thirteen Federal Judicial Circuits. *See* 28 U.S.C.A. § 41

Ninth Circuit. We have 11 numbered circuits, one for the District of Columbia, and one called the "Federal Circuit" that primarily handles patent matters. (See Figure 3–4 for a map of the thirteen federal judicial circuits.)

A litigant who loses in a federal circuit may then attempt to appeal the adverse decision to the U.S. Supreme Court. However, the Supreme Court generally has the discretion to determine which cases it accepts for review and which it does not. When it accepts a case for review it "grants *certiorari*" (*certiorari* is a Latin word meaning "to be informed of"). If it refuses to take the case, as it does approximately 95 percent of the time, it "denies *certiorari.*"

While there are federal courts other than those discussed here (tax courts, military justice courts, and bankruptcy courts, for example), this text addresses citation form for the most commonly encountered federal cases. Use Table T.1 of the *Bluebook* to determine citation form for cases from federal courts other than those discussed herein.

Citation of Federal Court Cases (Table T.1)

District Court Cases

Ordinarily, trial court cases in this country are not published. There are simply too many of them. West, however, decided to create a set of books to publish some cases from the district courts (the trial courts in our federal system) because important federal or constitutional issues may be raised in such cases. The set West created is called the *Federal Supplement* (abbreviated as "F. Supp." or F. Supp. 2d"). It is unofficial, and there are no parallel citations for cases from the federal district courts. Every citation, however, must include a reference to the specific deciding court, so include the district court information in the parenthetical with the date.

Examples:

Corey v. Shea, 889 F. Supp. 16 (E.D. Va. 1987).

Joshua Tree Ltd. v. Baker, 10 F. Supp. 2d 190 (S.D.N.Y. 1999).

Courts of Appeals Cases

At present, there is only one set of books that publishes cases from the intermediate courts of appeals: *Federal Reporter* (abbreviated as "F.," "F.2d," or "F.3d"), an unofficial set published by West. Thus, you need not worry about parallel citations for cases from the intermediate courts of appeals. Every citation, however, must include a reference to the specific deciding court, so always include the circuit information in the parenthetical with the date.

Examples:

Ray v. Libby Co., 789 F.2d 118 (2d Cir. 1994).

Atl. Mgmt. Co. v. Moe, 15 F.3d 931 (Fed. Cir. 1998).

U.S. Supreme Court Cases

Cases from the U.S. Supreme Court are published in a variety of sources. They are published officially in a set called *United States Reports*, and they are published unofficially in three places: by West in a set called *Supreme Court Reporter*, by Lawyers Co-operative in a set called *Lawyer's Edition* (or *Lawyer's Edition, Second Series*), and in a weekly journal called *U.S. Law Week*. Additionally, most U.S. Supreme Court cases can be located on the Internet.

Although there are thus at least four parallel citations for U.S. Supreme Court cases, the *Bluebook* rule is direct: cite to *United States Reports* (U.S.) if the case is published in that set. If not, cite to *Supreme Court Reporter* (S. Ct.), *Lawyer's Edition* (L. Ed. or L. Ed. 2d), or *U.S. Law Week* (U.S.L.W.) in that order of preference. Do not give a parallel citation.

If you are wondering why a case would not be published in the official *United States Reports*, remember that the set is official. It is published under government authority. The commercial publishers release volumes much more quickly. Thus, for newer cases, the official citation may not yet be available, requiring you to cite to one of the other sets.

Examples:

Farley v. Galloway, 501 U.S. 699 (1998).

Hall v. Porter, 239 S. Ct. 993 (2000).

The second citation would be for a case not yet published in the official *United States Reports.*

Practice Tip:

✓ Some practitioners use the form *Taylor v. Green,* ___ U.S. ___, 241 S. Ct. 90 (2000) for recent cases, presumably to indicate to a reader that while an official citation will eventually exist, it is not available yet, and thus the author is providing the reader with the "default" citation from the *Supreme Court Reporter.* Although this technique is commonly encountered in practice, there is no authority for it in the *Bluebook.* Check your firm or company practice.

Figure 3–5 provides a diagram of the federal court system.

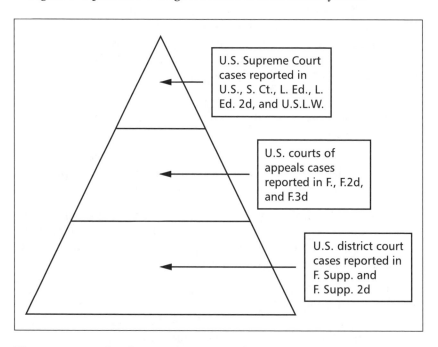

U.S. Supreme Court cases reported in U.S., S. Ct., L. Ed., L. Ed. 2d, and U.S.L.W.

U.S. courts of appeals cases reported in F., F.2d, and F.3d

U.S. district court cases reported in F. Supp. and F. Supp. 2d

Figure 3–5   Federal Court System (excluding administrative and specialized courts)

Public Domain Citations

Although the ABA has recommended a public domain citation system for federal cases, such a system has not been mandated by any federal courts. The use of a public domain citation is optional in the Sixth Circuit (covering Kentucky, Michigan, Ohio, and Tennessee). Most federal courts, however, adamantly oppose such citations. Thus, until further change is announced, follow the *Bluebook* and the examples herein. A citation from the Sixth Circuit would be *Allen v. Gray*, 1999 FED App. 0184P (6th Cir.). (See example in Table T.1 of the *Bluebook*.) Further discussion of the topic is found in Chapter 6.

SUBSEQUENT AND PRIOR HISTORY (RULE 10.7, TABLE T.9)

Subsequent History

When you "Shepardize" a case to determine whether it is still good law, you will find the subsequent history and treatment of the case as later courts or cases have discussed it. According to *Bluebook* Rule 10.7, you are ethically obligated to give the entire subsequent history of a case. Nevertheless, omit the following subsequent history:

- Denials of *certiorari* or denials of similar discretionary appeals, unless your case is less than two years old or the denial is particularly relevant.

- History on remand (when a case is returned or remanded to a trial court by an appellate court to ensure the lower court complies with the appellate court's instructions), unless relevant.

- Denials of discretionary appeals, such as rehearings (when a disappointed party requests that a court reconsider or rehear a case), unless relevant. Because rehearings are so often requested and seldom granted, generally omit this information.

Until the Sixteenth Edition of the *Bluebook* in 1996, one was always required to include a denial of *certiorari*. The Sixteenth and Seventeenth Editions of the *Bluebook* instruct writers to omit such denials unless the case is recent (less than two years old) or the denial is particularly relevant. Some practitioners object to the new rule, believing that the denial of *certiorari* sends a signal to a reader that a case is final and is, thus, always relevant. Determine if your firm or company has a policy regarding this matter.

How does one indicate subsequent history? When you Shepardize the case and find the subsequent history, consult Table T.9 of the *Bluebook* for the appropriate abbreviation and then cite as follows:

Examples:

Young v. Barr Co., 45 F.3d 18 (D.C. Cir. 1998), *cert. denied,* 520 U.S. 166 (1999). (Note: If underscoring, use a solid unbroken line for <u>cert. denied.</u>)

Jacobs v. Nelson, 789 F. Supp. 16 (D.N.J. 1994), *rev'd,* 904 F.2d 18 (3d Cir. 1995).

Practice Tip:

✓ If the date in the second parenthetical will be the same as that in the first, strike the date from the first parenthetical and retain it only in the second (Rule 10.5(d)) as follows:

Li v. Li, 44 F.3d 21 (9th Cir.), *aff'd,* 519 U.S. 901 (1998).

Prior History

Virtually all cases from the U.S. Supreme Court (and the highest courts in a state) have prior history because they were not originally decided by the Supreme Court but came to the Court from lower appellate courts. Are you required to give the prior history of such a case or other cases with prior history? No. Only give prior history if it is significant to the point you are making.

SERIES OF COURT REPORTS

You may have noticed that some citations are to "F.," while others are to "F.2d" or "F.3d." Similarly, some citations are to "N.E." while others are to "N.E.2d." Why? As publishers publish cases in the court reports, the volume numbers of the sets keep increasing. Probably to ensure that the volume number does not become confusingly high, the publishers eventually stop publishing an initial set (such as F. or N.E.) and begin publishing a new series (such as F.2d or N.E.2d). Still other sets can have higher series numbers such as Cal. 4th. You do not need to know when the series numbers switch over. You need only know that any case in F.3d is newer than any case in F.2d, and likewise any case in F.2d is newer than any case in F.

Note that the abbreviation for "second" in legal writing is always "2d" (rather than the nonlegal abbreviation "2nd" that is commonly used). Similarly, the abbreviation for "third" in legal writing is always "3d" and not "3rd." Other abbreviations, such as those for 4th, 5th, and so forth are identical to those used in nonlegal writing.

SPACING IN CITATIONS (RULE 6.1(a))

The following spacing rules apply to all citations, not merely cases. There are three spacing rules:

- If a single capital letter is followed by another single capital letter, close them up together with no spaces (for purposes of this rule, numerals and ordinals are treated as single capitals) and close up initials in personal names.

  A.2d   S.W.   U.S.   F.3d   N.W.2d   A.L.R.5th   J.C. Jones

- Multiple letter abbreviations (such as "Cal." and "Supp.") are preceded and followed by spaces.

  Cal. App.   F. Supp. 2d   So. 2d   S. Ct.   D. Minn.

- Be careful with the abbreviations for periodicals. The spacing rule requires you to determine if one or more of the capitals refers to the name of an entity, such as a school. If so, set the capital or capitals referring to the entity apart from other single capitals. Because this rule is so confusing, you should simply consult Table T.14, which gives abbreviations for more than 700 periodicals, and mimic the spacing you see. (Note, however, that you must convert the large and small capitals to ordinary roman type.)

  N.C. L. Rev.   N.M. L. Rev.

Exercise for Chapter 3

Correct the following citations. You may need to supply or create missing information. There may be more than one thing wrong with the citation.

Case Names

1. John Oliver versus T.J. Younger

   _____

2. H.L. Keane, Jr. Vs. Susan Jones, Ann Edwards, and Raymond Harris

   _____

3. State of Minnesota V. Baker Automobile Corporation (Assume citation appears as a "stand-alone" and is a Minnesota case.)

   _____

4. USA v. Franklin Liability Indemnity Company (Cite first assuming citation appears in a textual sentence, and then cite as a stand-alone citation.)

   _____

   _____

5. Jacob and Pamela Iverson versus Central Intelligence Agency

   _____

State Court Cases

6. Gray v. Gray, 692 Michigan 16. (Assume citation appears in a brief submitted to a Michigan court.)

   _____

7. Bradley v. Browning, 201 Cal. 2d 192, 78 California Reporter 14, 451 Pacific Reporter (Second Series) 16 (1998). (Assume citation appears in a brief submitted to a California court.)

   _____

8. Bradley v. Browning, 201 Cal. 2d 192, 78 California Reporter 14, 451 Pacific Reporter (Second Series) 16 (1998). (Assume citation appears in a letter to an adversary.)

---

9. Walters v. Barry Redmond, an Oklahoma case decided in 1990.

Federal Cases and Subsequent History

10. Bennett v. Bianco, 429 United States 16, 201 Supreme Court Reporter 12, 309 Lawyers' Edition, Second, 436 (1990).

---

11. Farley v. State of Arizona, a 2000 Third Circuit case located in volume 401 of the Federal Reporter (Third Series) at page 19. (Assume *certiorari* was granted for this case by the Supreme Court in 2000.)

---

12. Hawken vs. Smith, 12 F. 3d 28 (1996). (Assume this case was reversed by the United States Supreme Court in 1997.)

---

13. Sanchez v. Barclay Bank of Miami, Florida, (1995) 903 Federal Supplement 892.

---

14. Powell v. Silvers, a case from the Eastern District of Virginia, decided in 1998 and affirmed by the Fourth Circuit Court of Appeals in 1999.

Spacing

15. 13 Federal Reporter (Third Series) 892 (1996).

---

16. 391 California Appellate Reports, Third Series, page 109 (1984).

---

17. Ellis v. Ellis, 390 United States Reports 90 (1985).

_____

18. Sands v. Victor, 201 N. C. 14, 301 S E. 2nd 19 (1989).

_____

19. 36 Boston College Law Review 19 (1990).

_____

20. 45 New York University Law Review 144 (1982).

_____

CHAPTER 4 Citation Form for Statutes, Legislative Materials, Uniform Acts, Court Rules, and Constitutions

STATUTES (RULE 12)

Federal Statutes

Introduction

Federal statutes are published in three separate sources. They are published officially in a set called the *United States Code*, and they are published unofficially by West in a set called *United States Code Annotated* and by Lawyers' Co-operative in a set called *United States Code Service*. The basic citation form is the same for each set.

A citation must include the following elements:

- Reference to the title within the set
- Reference to the name of the set
- Citation to the relevant statutory section
- Parenthetical that includes a date and, if you cite to anything other than the official set, a reference to the publisher of the unofficial set

Thus, a reference to "17 U.S.C. § 107 (1996)" directs a reader to title 17 of the *United States Code*, section 107.

Examples:

35 U.S.C. § 101 (1996).

35 U.S.C.A. § 101 (West 1994).

35 U.S.C.S. § 101 (Law. Co-op. 1996).

State Statutes

Most of the 50 states and the District of Columbia refer to their statutes merely by title, chapter, and section numbers. Consult Table T.1 for the blueprint for each state jurisdiction (but remember to convert the typeface from large and small capitals to ordinary roman type).

Examples:

Colo. Rev. Stat. Ann. § 7-101-101 (West 19xx).

Neb. Rev. Stat. Ann. § 13-201 (Michie 19xx).

Ohio Rev. Code Ann. § 1701.01 (Anderson 19xx).

Some states, however, generally the more populous ones, have so many statutes that they are categorized into separately named titles. Once again, follow the format provided for each state in Table T.1.

Examples:

Cal. Evid. Code § 52 (West 19xx).

Md. Code Ann., Educ. § 16–148 (19xx).

N.Y. Bus. Corp. Law § 694 (McKinney 19xx).

Miscellaneous Information

Date

According to *Bluebook* Rule 12.3.2, the date that is placed in the parenthetical is not the date the statute was enacted but rather the date found on the spine of the book, the year appearing on the title page, or the latest copyright year, in that order of preference.

Pocket Parts (Rule 3.2(c))

If you located your statute in a pocket part or soft-cover supplement to the main volume, indicate such in the parenthetical as follows:

15 U.S.C.A. § 1051 (West Supp. 1998).
11 U.S.C.S. § 301 (Law. Co-op. 1996 & Supp. 1998). (Note: Parenthetical indicates that the statute is located both in the hardback main volume as well as in the pocket part.)

Practice Tips:

✓ Practitioners seldom include the parenthetical even though it is required by the *Bluebook*. Nearly all practitioners merely end their statutory citations after giving the section number of the statute, as in 35 U.S.C. § 601. Information in the parenthetical about the publisher of an unofficial set is particularly confusing due to the merging of many legal publishing companies. The *Bluebook*'s Table T.1 refers to some publishers who no longer publish the sets indicated. To determine the publisher whose name should be inserted in a parenthetical, check the copyright page of the set of statutes you use.

Spacing (Rule 6.2(c))

Follow the spacing rules given in Chapter 3 and place adjacent single capitals next to each other with no spaces between them. Always place a space after a section symbol (§) just as you would hit the space bar if you were typing the word "section."

Multiple Sections (Rule 3.4(b))

If you wish to direct the reader to several sections, give inclusive section numbers (separated by a hyphen) and use two section symbols with no spaces between them. If using a hyphen or dash would be ambiguous, use the word "to." Do not drop digits because statutes can be numbered so oddly that on encountering the reference "42 U.S.C. §§ 101-04," a reader might think he or she was being directed to a statute called "section 101, subdivision 4," rather than being directed to read sections 101 through 104. Thus, the correct form is "42 U.S.C. §§ 101-104 (1996)" or "Ga. Code Ann. §§ 14-2-101 to 14-2-114 (1997)." Similarly, do not use the expression "et seq." (meaning "and following") to direct a reader to several sections because it is too imprecise.

Section Symbol (Rule 6.2(c))

In citations, use the section symbol § rather than the word "section" except for the first word of a sentence, which can never be a symbol. Thus, state "Section 107 provides a complete defense" rather than "§ 107 provides a complete defense."

Odds and Ends

- Cite to the official code whenever possible (Rule 12.2.1(a)).

- In citations to the Internal Revenue Code, the reference to the title ("26 U.S.C.") may be replaced with "I.R.C." Thus, "26 U.S.C. § 101 (1996)" may be replaced with "I.R.C. § 101 (1996)" (Rule 12.8.1).

- If a statute is known by a popular name, that name may be used with the citation if it would be helpful. For example, "Lanham Act § 44(e), 15 U.S.C. § 1944(e) (1996)" is correct (Rule 12.3.1).

- The *Bluebook* gives little guidance regarding the spacing for parenthetical portions of statutes but generally shows no spacing. Thus, cite "17 U.S.C. § 106(a)" rather than "17 U.S.C. 106 (a)."

See the Appendix, Examples of State Cases and Statutes, for sample citations for all states and the District of Columbia.

LEGISLATIVE MATERIALS (RULE 13)

On occasion, legal writers discuss the history of certain statutes. For example, they may wish to compare the various versions of a bill, provide background about the intent of the statute according to its sponsor, or quote from floor debates. The material considered during the legislative process is called *legislative history* and may consist of versions of the bill, transcripts of committee hearings held to discuss the bill, committee reports issued after the hearings were held, or floor debates. Although there are other documents making up legislative history (joint resolutions, committee prints, and so forth), only the most commonly cited materials are discussed here.

Following are forms for federal legislative documents. Consult the *Bluebook* for information on citing state legislative documents. State legislative history is cited far less frequently than federal legislative history. Legislative history is not binding on a court. Like secondary authorities (discussed in Chapter 5), it is persuasive, not mandatory.

Bills (Rule 13.2)

Bills are introduced in either the House of Representatives or Senate during a congress. Each congress lasts two years and has two sessions, a first and a second. The first session always occurs in odd-numbered years while the second session always occurs in even-numbered years.

The 106th Congress began in January 1999. The 107th Congress begins in January 2001.

Cite bills as follows:

- H.R. 604, 105th Cong. § 3 (1998). This citation signals that the bill was the 604th piece of legislation introduced in the House of Representatives during the 105th Congress and that it was introduced in the second session (the year 1998 conveys this information). It directs the reader to section three of the bill.

- S. 90, 104th Cong. § 1 (1995). This citation references the 90th bill introduced in the Senate in the first session of the 104th Congress and directs the reader to section one of the bill.

Once the bill has been signed by the president, it is a law and should be cited as a statute, namely to U.S.C., U.S.C.A., or U.S.C.S.

Committee Hearings (Rule 13.3)

After a bill is introduced, it is sent to a committee, which will then hold hearings regarding the proposed legislation. Various parties may testify in favor of or against the bill. Transcripts of the committee hearings are published, and citations include the following information: entire title as it appears on the cover of the transcript (treat this title as a book title and, thus, either underscore or italicize it) bill number, committee or subcommittee name (using abbreviations in Tables T.6 and T.10), particular Congress, page of the transcript you wish the reader to review, and year of publication. If you wish, you may identify the witness who testified by using a parenthetical.

Cite committee hearings as follows:

Regulation of the Internet: Hearing on H.R. 114
Before the Senate Comm. on Commerce,
106th Cong. 19 (1999) (statement of Stanley Smith,
President, NTI Networks, Inc.).

Committee Reports (Rule 13.4)

After hearings are held, the committee issues a report giving its recommendations regarding the legislation. Citations to committee reports identify which house issued the report, number of the Congress connected by a hyphen to the number of the report, part or page to which the reader is directed, and year of publication.

Cite committee reports as follows:

- H.R. Rep. No. 105-42, at 16 (1998).
- S. Rep. No. 106-442, pt. 3, at 36 (1999).

Floor Debates (Rule 13.5)

A more or less verbatim transcript of debates occurring on the floor of the House of Representatives and Senate is published in the *Congressional Record,* a pamphlet published each day Congress is in session. These pamphlets, called daily editions, are eventually replaced by hardbound permanent volumes. When citing to a daily edition, give the full date (using abbreviations shown in Table T.13). Cite to volume, set, page, and date. If desired, you may identify the speaker.

Cite floor debates as follows:

- 135 Cong. Rec. 1911 (1985) (statement of Sen. Thurmond).
- 142 Cong. Rec. H401 (daily ed. Oct. 15, 1990) (statement of Rep. Wolfe). (Note: The "H" preceding "401" indicates that the statements can be found in the House section of the daily edition.)

UNIFORM ACTS (RULE 12.8.4)

Uniform acts are drafted with the intent they will be adopted by all states. There are approximately 200 uniform acts, the best known of which is the Uniform Commercial Code. Some states adopt the uniform act as drafted, while others make some changes to the act. A reference to a uniform law adopted by a state is cited just as any other statute from that state. West publishes a set entitled *Uniform Laws Annotated,* Master Edition, which publishes more than 160 uniform acts together with related information.

Examples:	
Uniform act:	U.C.C. § 2-316 (1977).
	Unif. Probate Code § 3-101 (1978).
State version of act:	Cal. Com. Code § 2-316 (West 1998).
Uniform Laws Annotated, Master Edition:	Unif. P'ship Act § 29, 14 U.L.A. 164 (1998).

COURT RULES (RULE 12.8.3)

Cite court rules of evidence or procedure as follows:

Examples:

Fed. R. Civ. P. 12(b)(3).

Fed. R. Crim. P. 40.

Fed. R. Evid. 210.

Cal. R. Ct. 97(b).

CONSTITUTIONS (RULE 11)

U.S. Constitution

Cite the United States Constitution as follows:

Examples:

U.S. Const. amend. XIV.

U.S. Const. art. I, § 8.

Remember to convert the large and small typeface you see in the *Bluebook* abbreviation of the word Constitution (CONST.) to ordinary roman type ("Const."). View the inside front and back covers of the *Bluebook* and compare the different presentation styles for law review footnotes and court documents.

State Constitutions

Cite to state constitutions by using the appropriate abbreviations for the states provided in Table T.11 and setting up the citation in a manner similar to that used for the United States Constitution.

Examples:

Cal. Const. art. XXII.

Nev. Const. art. II, § 4, cl. 6.

Practice Tip:

✓ It may look odd to see a lowercase "a" used for "amend." and "art." when referring to constitutions, but that is the rule. Do not give any date if the constitutional provision is still in force.

Exercise for Chapter 4

Correct the following citations. You may need to supply missing information.

1. Fifth Amendment to the U.S. Constitution.

2. Article 2, Section 1, clause 4, of the U.S. Constitution.

3. Article V of the New Mexico Constitution.

4. House of Representatives bill number 1209, 106th Congress.

5. Statement of Senator Dole, volume 139 of the Congressional Record, at page 190.

6. Judicial Nominations: Hearing on Senate Bill No. 901 before the Senate Judiciary Committee, held during the 105th Congress, Statement of Lawrence V. McConnell, Judge, Central District of California.

7. Title 11, Section 311 of the United States Code.

8. Section 981 of Title 35 of United States Code Annotated. (Assume the statute is found in the pocket part.)

9. 42 United States Code Service Sections 303 to 307 (1996).

---

10. Idaho Code Sections 30-1-1 to 30-1-14.

---

11. Delaware Code, title 8, section 155.

---

12. Maryland Code, Corporations and Associations, Sections 3-700 to 3-709.

---

13. California Streets and Highways Section 1440.

---

14. Uniform Commercial Code Section 2-201.

---

15. Federal Rule of Civil Procedure 53 (a).

---

16. House of Representatives Report Number 106-09, page 24.

CHAPTER 5 Secondary Sources

INTRODUCTION

Sources other than cases, constitutions, statutes, and administrative regulations are called *secondary sources* and include books, articles, and encyclopedias. Legal writers prefer to cite to primary sources rather than secondary sources because primary sources are mandatory (meaning courts must follow relevant primary sources), while secondary sources are persuasive at best. Note that the examples given in the *Bluebook* for many of the secondary authorities show large and small capitals. As always, practitioners should convert this form to ordinary roman style.

BOOKS AND TREATISES (RULE 15)

Cite books, pamphlets, and other nonperiodical materials by including the following:

- Volume number (if it is a multivolume work).

- Author (and editor and/or translator if one is given) set forth as the author himself or herself does, including any designation such as "Jr." or "IV." If there are two authors, list them both in the order given in the publication using an ampersand, as in "Leigh Peters & Sofia Bianco." If there are more than two authors, list only the first followed by the signal "et al." (meaning "and others") unless inclusion of all authors is relevant, in which case you may identify them all.

- Title of book (underscored or italicized, depending on preference) given as it appears on the title page. Note that some titles include the author's name, as in *McCarthy on Trademarks and Unfair Competition.* Do not put any punctuation after a book title.

- Page, section, or paragraph, dropping repetitious digits for pages (Rule 3.3(d)), but not for sections or paragraphs (Rule 3.4(b) and (c)).

- Parenthetical information (including any editor or translator, edition of the book if there is more than one edition, and year of publication).

Examples:

- 2 J. Thomas McCarthy, *McCarthy on Trademarks and Unfair Competition* § 4-13 (4th ed. 1998).

- 7 Samuel Williston, *Treatise on the Law of Contracts* § 901 (Walter H. Jaeger ed., 3d ed. 1964).

- Sandra Dolan, *Antitrust Law* § 4.06 (Anna Nelson trans., 4th ed. 1997).

- John Harris et al., *Indemnity Protection* ¶¶ 101-106 (1997).

PERIODICAL MATERIALS (RULE 16)

The publications that law schools periodically produce are generally called *law reviews.* Other periodical publications, such as the *Banking Law Journal,* are published to keep practitioners current in their chosen fields. Law reviews and law journals are frequently cited in court documents because they offer scholarly examinations of various legal topics.

A citation to a periodical generally includes the following:

- Author's full name as used by the author (follow the rules noted previously regarding multiple authors).

- Title of article written (underscored or italicized) and followed by a comma.

- Reference to periodical in which the article is published (cite to volume, set, and page, following the spacing and abbreviations shown in Table T.14).

- Year (given in parentheses).

Examples:

David J. Hayes, Jr., *Due Process,* 41 Emory L.J. 164 (1995).

Janet R. Sanders, *Juvenile Justice,* 77 Mass. L. Rev. 180 (1995).

Franklin Nelson & Taylor Luce, *The Common Law,* 13 J. Legal Educ. 245 (1990).

DICTIONARIES (RULE 15.7)

There are several law dictionaries. They are cited according to the rules governing books and treatises. Give the name of the book, page on which the definition appears, and parenthetical with the edition (if other than the first edition) and year of publication.

Examples:

Black's Law Dictionary 905 (7th ed. 1999).

Ballentine's Law Dictionary 54 (3d ed. 1969).

ENCYCLOPEDIAS (RULE 15.7)

Encyclopedias provide an easy-to-read overview of hundreds of legal topics. There are two national sets (*Corpus Juris Secundum* and *American Jurisprudence,* Second Series) and about ten state-specific sets. Although the explanations of the law are articulate and easy to understand, because their approach is so elementary, encyclopedias are seldom cited in authoritative legal writing. Their citation form includes the following elements:

- Volume number
- Reference to name of set
- Topic name (underscored or italicized)
- Section number
- Year (in parentheses)

Examples:

76 Am. Jur. 2d *Trademarks* § 63 (1994).

95 C.J.S. *Venue* § 4 (Supp. 1998). (Note: Parenthetical indicates that the information is found in the pocket part.)

14 Cal. Jur. 2d *Contracts* §§ 14-16 (1994).

RESTATEMENTS (RULE 12.8.5)

The *Restatements*, the product of the American Law Institute, aim to restate the law of a particular topic in a clear and concise fashion. Comments and notes on the use of the *Restatements* follow each articulation of any legal principle. The *Restatements* are likely the most highly regarded of the secondary authorities and are frequently cited.

Cite to the name of the *Restatement*, section number, reference to comment (if applicable), and year of publication.

Examples:

Restatement (Second) of Torts § 13 (1986).

Restatement (Second) of Contracts § 84 cmt. a (1986).

A.L.R. ANNOTATIONS (RULE 16.6.5)

Scholarly essays or annotations are published in *American Law Reports* on a variety of legal topics and are sufficiently respected that they are often cited in court documents and legal memoranda.

Citations include the following elements:

- Author's full name
- The word "Annotation" followed by a comma
- Title of the work (underscored or italicized) and followed by a comma
- Reference to volume, set, and page
- Year (in parentheses)

Examples:

James W. Gray, Annotation, *Nuisance Theory,* 56 A.L.R.4th 145 (1990).

Lindsey Goodman, Annotation, *Defenses in Discrimination Cases,* 64 A.L.R. Fed. 909 (1996).

Practice Tip:

✓ Never cite to a digest. Digests such as West's *Federal Practice Digest* or the *American Digest System* published by West are used as case finders. They help one find the law. They are neither primary nor secondary law themselves and, thus, can never be cited.

Exercise for Chapter 5

Correct the following citations. You may need to supply missing information.

1. The definition of "negligence" appearing on page 609 of Black's Law Dictionary.

---

2. Volume 2 of the third edition of a book written by Gary Richards, entitled "Copyright and Computers," Sections 16 through 18.

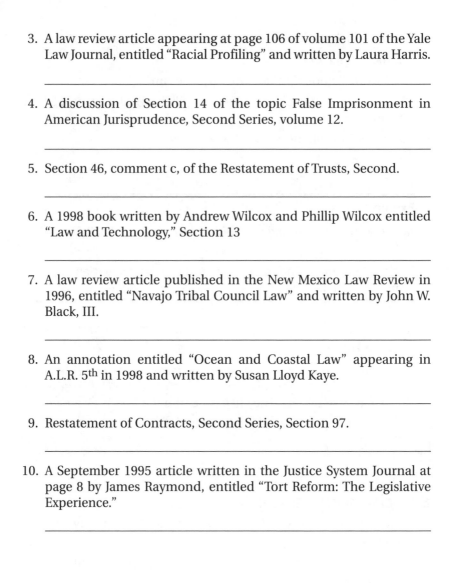

3. A law review article appearing at page 106 of volume 101 of the Yale Law Journal, entitled "Racial Profiling" and written by Laura Harris.

---

4. A discussion of Section 14 of the topic False Imprisonment in American Jurisprudence, Second Series, volume 12.

---

5. Section 46, comment c, of the Restatement of Trusts, Second.

---

6. A 1998 book written by Andrew Wilcox and Phillip Wilcox entitled "Law and Technology," Section 13

---

7. A law review article published in the New Mexico Law Review in 1996, entitled "Navajo Tribal Council Law" and written by John W. Black, III.

---

8. An annotation entitled "Ocean and Coastal Law" appearing in A.L.R. 5th in 1998 and written by Susan Lloyd Kaye.

---

9. Restatement of Contracts, Second Series, Section 97.

---

10. A September 1995 article written in the Justice System Journal at page 8 by James Raymond, entitled "Tort Reform: The Legislative Experience."

CHAPTER 6 Administrative Materials, Electronic Databases, The Internet, Record Materials, and Public Domain Citations

ADMINISTRATIVE MATERIALS (RULE 14)

In general, administrative materials consist of the rules, regulations, and other materials of federal administrative agencies (such as the SEC or FCC) and various executive materials, such as presidential proclamations and executive orders.

Agency Law

Federal agencies have the power to make rules and regulations, which, if properly promulgated, have the effect of statutes. Moreover, the agencies have the power to issue decisions to enforce their rules. The rules and regulations first appear in a daily pamphlet called the *Federal Register*. The regulations are then codified or organized into 50 titles (highly similar to the arrangement of the *United States Code*), and produced in a set published yearly called the *Code of Federal Regulations*. If the agencies are called on to adjudicate a controversy, the decision may be published in various case reports.

Rules and Regulations (Rule 14.2)

Cite rules and regulations to the *Code of Federal Regulations* (C.F.R.) whenever possible, giving the title, set name, section or part, and year (giving the year is critical because a new set of C.F.R. is published each year). If the regulation has a commonly known name, give it before the citation.

Examples:

18 C.F.R. § 701.254 (1998).

Cheese Import Regulations, 42 C.F.R. § 131 (1999).

Cite to the *Federal Register* only when the regulation has not yet been published in C.F.R., in which case give also any commonly used name of the regulation. Further, if the *Federal Register* indicates where the regulation will appear in C.F.R., give that information parenthetically. Citations to the *Federal Register* include the volume, set, page number, and exact date.

Examples:

Standard Industrial Codes, 64 Fed. Reg. 278 (Dec. 6, 1997).

Federal Contract Regulations for Small Businesses, 60 Fed. Reg. 1801 (Mar. 9, 1998) (to be codified at 22 C.F.R. pt. 120).

Treasury Regulations (Rule 14.5.1)

Treasury regulations are not cited to C.F.R. Use the following form: Treas. Reg. § 42.26(b) (1989).

Administrative Decisions (Rule 14.3)

Official Reporters

Decisions issued by various agencies may be published in the official reporters of the agency. Cite to the official reporter if the decision is found therein. Those reporters (and their correct abbreviations) are listed in Table T.1 of the *Bluebook* (before the instructions given for each state). Cite to (and underscore or italicize) the full reported name of the first-listed private party (namely, a party that is not an agency of the government) or the official subject-matter title, volume number, set name, page or paragraph, and year of decision (given in parentheses).

Examples:

Network Solutions, Inc., 18 F.C.C.2d 909 (1998).

Stevens Textiles Co., 403 N.L.R.B. 120, 124 (1995).

Looseleaf Services (Rule 19)

Not every agency publishes its cases officially. A variety of private publishers (notably Commerce Clearing House, Clark Boardman Callaghan, and Bureau of National Affairs) publish cases and other administrative materials unofficially in sets of binders called "looseleaf services." "Looseleaf" refers to the fact that as new material is released, old pages are taken out of the binders and the new pages are inserted. In some instances, the looseleaf binders are later replaced by bound volumes. For example, the *Business Franchise Guide* includes cases, statutes, administrative regulations, and a host of other information relating to franchise law. Generally, cite decisions in looseleaf services as follows: case name (underscored or italicized), volume, abbreviated title of set, publisher (in parentheses), reference to paragraph or section, court information and date (in parentheses, giving exact date for material found in a looseleaf service and the year only for material found in a bound volume). Older materials or materials awaiting binding may be kept in semipermanent "transfer binders." Table T.16 in the *Bluebook* provides a list of the most frequently cited looseleaf services, giving their proper abbreviations. If a set is not listed in Table T.16, use Table T.14 to locate appropriate abbreviations so you can construct a title.

Examples:

In re Walmart Stores, Inc., 5 Bus. Franchise Guide (CCH) ¶ 42,201 (D.N.J. Aug. 12, 1995).

Davidson Co. v. Emory Inst., 24 Communications Reg. (P & F) ¶ 9019 (S.D.N.Y. May 1,1997).

In re Sav-All Drug Co., 6 Bankr. L. Rep. (CCH) ¶ 66,180 (Bankr. D. Or. 1995).

In re Jacobs, [1994–1995 Transfer Binder] Fed. Sec. L. Rep. (CCH) ¶ 12,021 (M.D. Pa. 1995).

Presidential and Executive Materials (Rule 14.7)

Presidents can issue proclamations (for action having no legal effect, such as declaring June 10, 1997 "Girl Scout Appreciation Day") or executive orders (which have the effect of law until a court rules otherwise). Most presidential material is published in title 3 of C.F.R. If the material is also published in U.S.C. (or U.S.C.A. or U.S.C.S), give that citation also. If the presidential material is so recent it is not yet in C.F.R., cite to the *Federal Register* and give exact date.

Examples:

Proclamation No. 4689, 3 C.F.R. 180 (1984).

Proclamation No. 4991, 50 Fed. Reg. 35,012 (Jan. 8, 1998).

Exec. Order No. 15,412, 50 Fed. Reg. 11,102 (Sept. 1, 2000).

Exec. Order No. 13,782, 3 C.F.R. 690 (1990), *reprinted in* 3 U.S.C. § 343 (1998).

LEXIS AND WESTLAW (RULE 18)

There are two major computerized legal research systems: Lexis (owned by Reed Elsevier Publishing Co.) and Westlaw (owned by West Group). Although there are some differences between the two systems, they are nearly equal in most respects. Many researchers enjoy using these computerized systems because they are easy to access and provide quick results. Of course, proficiency takes time and practice. The question then becomes, how does one cite to material located via Lexis or Westlaw?

The Seventeenth Edition of the *Bluebook* continues a prejudice against citing to the commercial electronic databases, primarily due to the variance in their availability and permanence. The *Bluebook* (Rule 18) requires the use and citation of traditional printed sources. Only when the material is not available in a printed source or when the traditional source is obscure or difficult to locate and citation to an electronic source will substantially improve access to the information should the electronic source be given. Even then, however, the traditional source should be cited and the Lexis or Westlaw (or other database) citation is given as a parallel citation. Nevertheless, the *Bluebook* acknowledges the reliability and authoritativeness of Lexis and Westlaw and prefers these electronic sources to the Internet. (See Rule 18.1.) Thus, only cite to an electronic database such as Lexis or Westlaw when the information is not available in a printed source or when use and citation of the traditional source is obscure or difficult. If a case is reported in conventional print materials, citation to Lexis or Westlaw would be inappropriate.

Similarly, for statutes Rule 12.2.1 states that one should cite statutes to the official code. If that is unavailable, one may cite to an unofficial code, official session laws, privately published session laws, widely used computer database, looseleaf service, an Internet source, or newspaper, *in that order of preference.* Thus, citing statutes to Lexis or Westlaw can be done only when a federal statute is unavailable in U.S.C., U.S.C.A., U.S.C.S., or any session laws.

Why is citation to electronic databases frowned on when the databases have been in existence for years? Some experts believe that citing to electronic databases makes retrieval difficult for many judges who either do not have access to Lexis or Westlaw in their courthouse chambers or are unskilled in the use of the electronic databases. Over time, this will likely change. For now, however, the general rule is that one should cite to Lexis or Westlaw only when the authority is not available in conventional print form or when the use and citation of the traditional source is particularly difficult.

For cases, cite as follows: case name, docket number of case, database identifier, and court name and exact date parenthetically. If screen or page numbers have been assigned, indicate such with an asterisk before the relevant number. (See Rule 18.1.1.)

Examples:

Cases   *Bowen Assoc. v. Capital Fin. Group,* No. 94-1765, 1995 U.S. App. LEXIS 1202, at *2 (4th Cir. Oct. 8, 1995).

> *Green v. Taylor,* No. 97-CAS-120, 1998 WL 44102,
> at *1 (D.N.J. Feb. 10, 1998).

Short Forms   *Bowen,* 1995 U.S. App. LEXIS 1202, at *3.

Green, 1998 WL 44102, at *2.

For statutes, cite to title, set, and section and then give parenthetically the name of the database and information relating to the currency of the database (rather than giving the year of the code). If the code is published unofficially, give the name of the publisher in the parentheses as well. (See Rule 18.1.2.)

Examples:

Statutes   42 U.S.C. § 1204 (LEXIS through 1998 Sess.).

Cal. Educ. Code § 155 (West, WESTLAW through 1997 Sess.).

S.D. Codified Laws § 21-103 (Michie, LEXIS through 1998 Reg. Sess.).

THE INTERNET (RULE 18.2)

If citing to the Internet, include the following: the available information about the authority being cited; an appropriate explanatory phrase (if any) to indicate which source you used; the party responsible for the Internet site (if not apparent from the Uniform Resource Locator, or URL); the URL; a date parenthetical; and any explanatory parenthetical. A URL is an Internet address, for example, www.uspto.gov. The *Bluebook* provides a thorough description of URLs in Rule 18.2.1(c).

The Seventeenth Edition continues the *Bluebook*'s preference for conventional print materials over electronic sources, primarily because the conventional print sources are more cite-worthy. Rule 18.2.1 provides that traditional printed sources should be used and cited except when the information is unavailable in a printed source or if the traditional printed source is obscure and hard to find and citation to the Internet will substantially improve access to the information. In the latter case, the traditional printed source should also be cited and the Internet citation is given as a parallel citation.

Thus, although there are thousands of cases and statutes available for viewing on the Internet, generally you cannot cite to them on the Internet because they are available in conventional print form. In fact, the *Bluebook* states that cases and statutes must be cited first to a traditional source or an electronic database (such as Lexis or Westlaw) except that an Internet source may be cited when the information is not available in a traditional source or electronic database. Nevertheless, if local rules permit or require citation to the Internet, those rules supersede the *Bluebook*.

When citing to the Internet, use the following explanatory phrases before the URL:

- *available at* (when using the Internet citation as a parallel citation)

- *at* (when the material is found exclusively on the Internet, such as in a journal published exclusively online)

No explanatory phrase is to be used when you accessed only the Internet source.

Date Information (Rule 18.2.1(e))

A citation that includes both a traditional source and a parallel Internet source should provide the date for the traditional source. If the date for the Internet source would be helpful, it may be given as well.

If the citation is only to the Internet source, a date must be provided before the URL for an online journal and after the URL in all other cases. The date provided should be one of the following (in this order of preference):

- The date of the case, statute, or article

- The date the Internet site was last modified

- The date the Internet site was last visited

If no date is given, indicate such as follows: (n.d.).

Examples:

Case published in print source but available on the Internet:
Feist Publ'ns Inc. v. Rural Tel. Serv. Co., 499 U.S. 340 (1991),

available at http://caselaw.findlaw.com/scripts/getcase.pl?
court=us&vol=499&invol.=340.

**Statute published in print source but accessed only through the
Internet:** 17 U.S.C. § 101 (1998), Cornell Legal Info. Inst.,
http://www4.law.cornell.edu/uscode/17/101.html.

**Article published in print source but accessed only through the
Internet:** Jonathan Hudis, *Trademarks in Cyberspace:
Gathering Your Evidence to Make a Difference*, 6 Multimedia &
Tech. Licensing L. Rep. 6 (2000), www.oblon.com/pub/seeker/
php3?hudis-tmcyber.html.

Article available only on the Internet: Brenda Sandburg, *PTO's
Destination: Silicon Valley* (last visited June 28, 1999), *at*
http://www.lawnewsnet.com/stories.

RECORD MATERIALS (P.7; TABLE T.8)

In many instances, legal writers wish to refer in a brief to other plead-
ings, motions, or materials that make up part of the court's record in a
case. For example, a plaintiff may wish to draw the court's attention to
an allegation made by the defendant in an answer to a complaint. The
Bluebook offers only minimal guidance.

Follow these citation tips:

- Enclose the reference in parentheses, putting a period inside the
  parentheses if the parenthetical reference stands alone at the end
  of a sentence and surrounding the parentheses with no punctuation if the reference appears as a clause within a sentence.

- You may string references together using semicolons.

- Use the abbreviations shown in Table T.8 of the *Bluebook*.

- Omit articles and prepositions from the title of a court document,
  unless confusion would result.

- Use "at" before a page number but not before a paragraph or section symbol.

- Ensure consistency in your citation form.

- Use the "hereinafter" form to establish an abbreviation of a long title described in text after you have cited the material in full the first time, as follows: "Juvenile Office Probation Sentencing Report" (hereinafter "Sentencing Report").

Example:

Defendant has alleged that he revoked his acceptance of the contract. (Def.'s Answer to Compl. ¶ 3.) Nevertheless, Defendant has acknowledged that the purported revocation was mailed to Plaintiff only after Plaintiff had signed and delivered the contract. (Def.'s Dep. at 26.) As discussed in Plaintiff's Motion for Summary Judgment (hereinafter "Motion") and other witnesses have confirmed (Attach. B at 4) the mailing of the revocation was effected only after execution and delivery of the contract by Plaintiff. (Gregson Decl. ¶ 14; Harrison Dep. at 62; Franklin Aff. Ex. A ¶ 3.)

PUBLIC DOMAIN CITATIONS (RULE 10.3.3; P.3)

Introduction

Ever-increasing numbers of cases and statutes have begun appearing on the Internet. However, the traditional method of citing to volume and page numbers in printed books of case reports cannot be used effectively for new opinions appearing on the Internet because the printed case books are not published for several weeks (or even months) after an opinion is released on the Internet. Therefore, both the American Bar Association (ABA) and the American Association of Law Libraries (AALL) have recommended that courts adopt a uniform citation system that is equally adaptable whether authorities are located in conventional printed materials or through electronic means. The Department of Justice has recommended that the federal courts adopt the ABA proposal to ensure consistency among the federal courts.

The proposed system is variously called "public domain," "vendor neutral," or "medium neutral" because the citation will look the same whether the source is found in print or electronic media. West, however, has called public domain citations "nowhere cite[s]," believing the citations do not refer readers to any actual, physical location for a case.

ABA Approach

In 1996, the ABA formally recommended to federal and state courts that they adopt a universal and medium neutral citation system. The ABA approach was largely patterned after the AALL solution. The ABA recommended that courts assign the citation at the time decisions are released to the public to enable readers to easily locate material whether they review the case in print form or on the Internet. Citations would include the following:

- Case name

- Year of decision

- Identification of court issuing the opinion

- Sequential number of the decision

- Reference to specific numbered paragraphs in which material is located

The ABA also recommended that citations include parallel citations until electronic publications become commonly used by practitioners and judges. The parallel citation would not include any pinpoint citations (that is, a reference to the specific page on which material appears).

Example:

Allen v. Rousch, 1998 4Cir. 24, ¶ 14, 35 F.3d 107.

The citation in this example tells the reader that the case name is *Allen v. Rousch,* that it was the 24th case decided in 1998 by the Fourth Circuit Court of Appeals, and that the reader is directed to paragraph 14 within the case. The parallel citation then tells the reader the case is located in volume 35 of the *Federal Reporter,* Third Series, beginning at page 107. The *Bluebook* (Table T.1) provides the following format: *Shea v. Wilson,* 1998 FED App. 218 (6th Cir.).

The *Bluebook* Approach (Rule 10.3.3; P.3)

Practitioners' Note P.3, in discussing parallel citations for state court cases, states that if a state court decision is available through an official public domain citation, that citation may be required instead of a traditional reporter, and a citation to a traditional source should be provided as well. *Bluebook* Rule 10.3.3 phrases this rule more authoritatively and flatly states that if it is available, a parallel citation to the appropriate regional reporter *must* be provided in addition to the public domain citation. Thus, the public domain citation really only replaces the official citation. The citation should include the case name, year of decision, the state's two character postal code (given in Table T.1), the court abbreviation (given in Table T.7) unless the court is the state's highest court, sequential number of the decision, an uppercase "U" if the decision is unpublished, and a paragraph number when referring to specific material in the case.

Example:

Wade v. Lee, 1997 ME 44, ¶ 15, 401 A.2d 909.

Which states have adopted official public domain citation formats such that you would use the format described herein rather than the usual approach consisting of case name, official citation, regional citation, and year of decision? At the time of publication of the Sixteenth Edition of the *Bluebook* in 1996, only Louisiana had adopted a public domain citation format. Since that time, Arizona, Colorado, Maine, Mississippi, Montana, New Mexico, North Dakota, Oklahoma, South Dakota, Utah, and Wisconsin have adopted public domain citation systems, and Arkansas, Florida, Georgia, and Tennessee are considering such adoption. If you cite cases from these states, check state and local court rules regarding citation form. In the absence of any information, follow the format shown in the *Bluebook.* Table T.1 provides an example for each of the above-listed states. Additional information can be located at the ABA's website, as follows: *ABA Legal Technology Resource Center, Uniform Citation Standards, at* www.abanet.org/citation/home.html (last visited June 14, 2000). The *Bluebook* itself suggests that information on jurisdictions adopting a public domain format since the publication of the Seventeenth Edition of the *Bluebook* in late 2000 can be found at http://www.legalbluebook.com.

There is much variation from state to state in spacing and abbreviations in these public domain citations. Some states neither underscore nor italicize case names in public domain citations. Additional information may be available at your state's home page. Access the website for the Georgetown Law Center law library (http://www.ll.georgetown.edu) and then select "state, local & territorial" law. When you are presented with a map of the United States, select your state and look for information about "judiciary." Information about citation form and other state-specific rules may be provided at the site. Additionally, Table T.1 provides references to each state's judicial website.

Note that the *Bluebook* discussion of public domain citations only relates to state court cases. There is no indication in the *Bluebook* that using a public domain citation for any federal case (other than one from the Sixth Circuit) is appropriate. In fact, most federal court judges are adamantly opposed to public domain citations, primarily because the burden of numbering paragraphs and assigning sequential opinion numbers would fall on the courts themselves. Nevertheless, the Sixth Circuit Court of Appeals has made the use of a public domain citation optional in the Sixth Circuit and an example is shown in Table T.1.

Exercise for Chapter 6

Correct each citation. You may need to supply or create missing information. Assume citations are "stand-alone" citations.

1. Plaintiff's Deposition, page 42   _____

    Defendant's Answer to Interrogatory, page 14   _____

    Exhibit A   _____

    Plaintiffs' Points and Authorities, Paragraph 14   _____

    Defendants' Counterclaim, Paragraph 16   _____

2. *Ott v. Park Development Co.*, volume 6, Labor Law Reports, Paragraph 1201.

    _____

3. Presidential Proclamation Number 5089. (Assume material is available in C.F.R.)

    _____

4. Executive Order 16,019. (Assume material is available in C.F.R.)

_____

5. Section 121.101 of title 29 of *Code of Federal Regulations.*

_____

6. *Brady v. Sanders,* No. 95-145, (11th Circuit May 9, 1996) LEXIS 907, U.S. App. 1996.

_____

7. Article by Person, Candace E., entitled "Citation of Legal and Non-legal Electronic Database Information" (last visited August 6, 1998) and located only at "http://www.michbar.org/publications/citation.htm."

_____

_____

_____

8. "Priority Watch List Determinations," volume 68 of *Federal Register,* page 1901, to be codified in title 33 of *Code of Federal Regulations* at part 200.

_____

_____

_____

9. Give public domain citations for the following:

    a. *Parker v. Bonette Agency Service, Co.,* the 201st case in 1999 from the Sixth Circuit. (Use *Bluebook* format.)

    _____

    b. *Talbot v. Taylor,* the 69th case in 1998 from the South Dakota Supreme Court, Paragraph 4 (also located at volume 505 of North Western Reporter, Second Series, at page 18).

    _____

CHAPTER 7 Punctuation, Quotations, Omissions, Alterations, and Parentheticals

PUNCTUATION FOR CITATIONS (RULE 1.4; P.2)

There are only three punctuation marks used after a citation is given: periods, commas, and semicolons. Use these marks as follows:

- Use a period to follow a citation when it supports or contradicts a previous declaratory sentence (P.2).

Example:

Trademarks can be abandoned through nonuse. *Gen. Cas. Constr. Co. v. Hart,* 482 U.S. 15 (1990). (Note: Such a citation ending with a period is a "stand-alone" citation, and thus, any of the more than 160 words in Table T.6 in the *Bluebook* may be abbreviated in the case name, including the first word in the case name.)

- Use a comma to follow a citation when the citation supports or contradicts only part of a sentence (P.2).

Example:

Although trademarks can be abandoned by nonuse, *General Casualty Construction Co. v. Hart,* 482 U.S. 15 (1990), evidence of nonuse must be clear and convincing. *Davis v. Kaye,* 483 U.S. 190 (1992).

- Use a semicolon to separate citations from each other when more than one citation supports or contradicts a previous statement, namely, when the citations are placed in a "string." (See Rule 1.4.) Note that the string is usually preceded by a signal such as *see, but see,* and so forth.

Practice Tip:

✓ String citing is disfavored by many judges who believe it clutters a document. Moreover, the rules relating to string citing are complex (Rule 1.4). The citations in a string must be placed in a hierarchical order. The most authoritative citation should be placed first. Thereafter, the citations must be placed according to the numerous rules of the *Bluebook*. For example, federal cases are placed before state court cases, state court cases are listed alphabetically by state (if there are several cases from the same state, those from higher courts precede those from lower courts), and cases from the same court are placed in reverse chronological order. Thus, Georgia Supreme Court cases are listed before Georgia appellate court cases, and if there are three Georgia appellate court cases, the most recent is listed first, followed by the next oldest, and so forth.

Example:

A general partnership agreement need not be in writing. *See Allen v. James Bus. Co.,* 433 F.2d 18 (8th Cir. 1990); *Hardy v. Oakland Co.,* 401 N.E.2d 18 (Mass. 1994); *Malone v. Midwestern Realty Org.,* 414 N.E.2d 89 (Mass. App. Ct. 1996); *Powell v. Lyden Co.,* 412 N.E.2d 149 (Mass. App. Ct. 1995).

QUOTATIONS (RULE 5)

Introduction—Pinpoint Cites

When quoting from an authority you must give the page on which the quotation appears. What if you are merely paraphrasing the authority rather than directly quoting from it? The *Bluebook* offers little help, merely stating, "[W]hen referring to specific material within . . . a source, include both the page on which the source begins and the page on which the specific material appears, separated by a comma" (Rule 3.3 (a)).

Example:

Copyrights are governed by federal law. *Wade v. Grayson,* 409 U.S. 14, 16 (1988); *Donoghue v. Cook,* 241 Va. 116, 120, 201 S.E.2d 409, 414 (1995).

The second page number is called a "pinpoint citation" because you are pinpointing for the reader exactly where to find material you are discussing. Occasionally, the second number is called a "jump citation," indicating you are asking the reader to jump to a certain page within a source.

The general practice is to always include the pinpoint citation, even if you are not directly quoting from a source. Why? It is the courteous approach, saving the reader from endlessly hunting through the authority trying to find the material you discuss. Moreover, if your research says what you claim it does, you should have no concern about allowing someone to verify your statements through the use of pinpoint citations. If a case has parallel citations, give the pinpoint citation for each.

Shorter Quotations (Rule 5.1(b))

If your quotation is 49 words or fewer, do not indent it. Merely keep the quotation in the regular portion of your narrative. Use quotation marks (" ") to designate which material is being quoted, and *always* place commas and periods inside the quotation marks, even if your quote is only one word long. Other punctuation marks should be placed inside your quotation marks only if they are part of the material quoted. Should you count the words in a quote to determine its length? Yes, absolutely; you should always count the words.

Example:

Courts have consistently held that while directors and officers of a corporation are not ordinarily liable for corporate obligations, this shield of limited liability will be pierced "when necessary to prevent fraud or injustice." *Carter v. Andrews Equip. Co.,* 482 U.S. 190, 194–95 (1995).

Lengthy Quotations (Rule 5.1(a))

A quotation that is 50 words or longer should be indented ten spaces left and right and single-spaced. Because the writing will appear as a chunk of words on the paper, this type of quotation is often referred to as a "block quotation." Do not use quotation marks for a block quotation. The fact that material is indented or blocked signals to the reader that it is a quotation.

Authors often place the citation for the quoted material within the indented block itself. This is incorrect. Only quoted material belongs in the block. The citation should be placed at the left margin on the first new line immediately following the block quotation (which appears two lines below the block quotation). If you then start a new paragraph, the citation may appear to be floating or hanging in space. Although odd-looking, this presentation is correct. Follow this format:

> Xxxxxxxxxxxxxxxxxxxxxxxxxxxxxxxxxxxxxxxxxxxxxxxxxxxxxxxxxxxxxx
> xxxxxxxxxxxxxxxxxxxxxxxxxxxxxxxxxxxxxxxxxxxxxxxxxxxxxxxxxxxxxx
> xxxxxxxxxxxxxxxxxxxxxxxxxxxxxxxxxxxxxxxxxxxxxxxxxxxxxxxxxxxxxx
> xxxxxxxxxxx

Lee v. Henry, 505 U.S. 6, 10 (1998).

Practice Tip:

✓ You often see legal writers block-indenting quotes that are fewer than 50 words. Generally, this is done for stylistic reasons, so that the material is more dramatically presented to the reader. Many judges, however, are sticklers for *Bluebook* rules, so using a block for a short quotation merely for drama purposes may be disfavored.

Odds and Ends

- **Showing Emphasis.** Do not use the expression "emphasis in original" if a word is italicized or otherwise emphasized in the original quotation. In legal writing, it is presumed that readers are sophisticated, and they will thus assume you have reproduced a quotation scrupulously. It is only when you change a quotation, perhaps by italicizing a word for emphasis, that you will indicate "emphasis added" (Rule 5.2). For example, the following is correct: The Court stated, "these limited liability partners are not personally liable for the acts of *misconduct* of their co-partners." *Randall v. Cox,* 500 U.S. 160, 165 (1994) (emphasis added). If you are underscoring rather than italicizing, use a solid unbroken line to show words you have emphasized.

- **Multiple Pages.** If a quotation spans more than one page, give the inclusive page numbers, separated by a hyphen or dash, retaining the last two digits, but striking other repetitious digits, as follows: *Nelson v. Nelson,* 601 P.2d 920, 922–26 (Wyo. 1995). (Rule 3.3(d)).

- **Quotation on First Page.** If the material you discuss or quote appears on the first page of a source, repeat the page, as follows: Guy Talbot, *Bankruptcy Preferences,* 37 How. L.J. 18, 18 (1990). (Rule 3.3(a)).

- **Quotations within Quotations.** In narrative text, if your quotation itself quotes from another source, switch from double quotation marks to single quotation marks to double quotation marks, and so forth (Rule 5.1(b)). In a block quotation, quotation marks should appear as they do in the original source (Rule 5.1(a)).

- **Nonconsecutive Pages.** If referring to nonconsecutive pages, set the citation up as follows: *Amey v. Scalise,* 502 U.S. 14, 18, 22 (1997). (Rule 3.3(d)).

- **Repeated References.** If a point is repeatedly made throughout a source, omit the pinpoint citation and use the word "*passim,*" which means "everywhere," as follows: *Marks v. Carson,* 506 U.S. 180 *passim* (1998). Note that there is no comma between the page number and *passim* (Rule 3.3(d)).

- **Paragraph Structure.** If a quotation you are indenting is a new paragraph in the original source, indicate such by also indenting the first line of your block quotation. If your block quotation includes several paragraphs from the original material, a blank line should separate each paragraph from the next and each paragraph within the block should be indented to mimic the paragraph structure of the original quote. Show the omission of an entire paragraph by four indented periods on a separate line (Rule 5.4).

Example:

    Xxxxxxxxxxxxxxxxxxxxxxxxxxxxxxxxxxxxx
xxxxxxxxxxxxxxxxxxxxxxxxxxxxxxxxxxxxxxxx
xxxxxxxxxxxxxxxxxxxxxxxxxxxxxxxxxxxxxxxx.

    . . . .

    Xxxxxxxxxxxxxxxxxxxxxxxxxxxxxxxxxxxxx
xxxxxxxxxxxxxxxxxxxxxxxxxxxxxxxxxxxxxxxx
xxxxxxxxxxxxxxxxxxxxxxxxxxx.

---

*   **Piggybacking.** If your quotation is originally from a case other than the one you are relying on, indicate such as follows: "Employers are vicariously liable for 'certain acts of their employees.'" *Edwards v. Lane,* 501 U.S. 294, 299 (1998) (quoting *O'Connor v. Schultz,* 450 U.S. 24, 27 (1990)). (Rule 5.2).

OMISSIONS (RULE 5.3)

It is acceptable to omit material from a quotation, as long as you indicate such. Use an *ellipsis* (three periods separated by spaces which are preceded and followed by spaces) to show omitted material.

Example:

"Punitive damages must be . . . based upon actual damages." *Harvey Ltd. v. Viacor, Inc.,* 451 U.S. 91, 97 (1990).

Follow these additional rules:

*   To show that you omitted material at the end of a sentence, use four periods (three for the ellipsis and one to show the period at the end of the sentence), as follows: "A landlord must provide habitable premises to a tenant . . . ." Note that a space is placed before the first period.

*   If you quote matter, then omit matter and quote additional material, set up the quotation as follows: "A corporation can be dissolved

by the state. . . . [A]n involuntary dissolution involves a court proceeding." Note that there is no space after the word "state" and before the first period. Why? You are telling the reader that you did not omit any part of the first sentence. Thus, you retain its original punctuation.

- If you are merely quoting a phrase within a sentence, you do not need an ellipsis. Set up such a quotation as follows: The Court further held that "sexual harassment is prohibited under Title VII" and is "a significant workplace problem."

- Never use an ellipsis to begin a quotation. Use a bracketed letter to show that language beginning a sentence has been omitted, as follows: "[I]t is axiomatic that damages are awarded for breach of contract." The placement of an uppercase "I" in the brackets shows that in the original quotation the "I" was a lowercase letter. This signals to the reader that the word "it" was not the first word of the sentence.

- It is acceptable to omit citations that appear in the middle of a quotation (generally because they clutter the quotation). Simply give your quotation and at the end include the phrase "citations omitted" in a parenthetical, as follows: "Consent is a defense to the tort of battery." *May v. Jeffers*, 681 P.2d 18, 25 (Wyo. 1994) (citations omitted).

ALTERATIONS (RULE 5.2)

An alteration is a minor change in a quote, such as changing a letter from upper- to lowercase (or vice versa), pluralizing or singularizing a word, changing a tense, correcting spelling, or adding a word. Use brackets to show alterations.

Example:

"[I]nfringement of trademarks can be shown by proof of [actual] confusion."

The use of the brackets in the preceding example tells the reader that in the original quotation the word "infringement" started with a lowercase "i" and that the word "actual" did not appear. Rather, the author inserted the word "actual" for purposes of style or readability.

Example:

"The landlord[s] failed to act in accordance with contractual duties."

The use of the brackets in this example tells the reader that in the original quotation the word "landlord" was singular. Here, the author wants to pluralize the word for purposes of style. An empty bracket in a word, for example, "action[ ]," tells the reader that in the original quotation there was another letter in the word (clearly, the word was "actions").

PARENTHETICALS (RULE 10.6)

Legal writers often use parenthetical expressions to convey certain information (other than dates). Generally, parentheticals fall into two categories.

* **Weight of Authority.** Some parentheticals tell the reader something about the strength or weakness of the citation. Some of the more frequently used parentheticals to show weight of authority are as follows: en banc, 5–4 decision, mem. (for memorandum decisions, namely those in which a court issues a holding but gives either no or very little opinion), per curiam (meaning "by the court," indicating an opinion in which no particular author is identified), and identifications of concurring and dissenting opinions.

Examples:

* The Court upheld the doctrine of equivalents. *Carley v. Bennett,* 404 U.S. 16, 19–21 (1985) (9–0 decision).

* The endorsement test should be used in First Amendment cases examining separation of church and state. *Sherman v. Carlson,* 410 U.S. 610, 646 (1987) (O'Connor, J., dissenting).

  Note: Readers will always assume you are relying on the majority opinion. Thus, if you rely on a dissenting or concurring opinion, indicate such by the use of a parenthetical.

- **Explanatory Parentheticals.** Explanatory parentheticals are those that provide some explanation about the case. They should be given after parentheticals that indicate the weight of authority but before any subsequent history. Note that the expression in the parenthetical begins with a present participle (a verb ending in "ing" such as "holding" or "rejecting") (Rule 1.5).

Remember that we have already discussed certain parenthetical expressions, namely the expressions "citations omitted," used when you wish to delete citations from the middle of your quotation and "piggybacking," used to indicate that your case relied on or quoted from an earlier case.

Examples:

- *Lowell v. Lynn,* 689 F.2d 191, 194-97 (D.C. Cir. 1990) (5–4 decision) (holding that trademarks can be diluted either by blurring or tarnishment).

- *Miller v. Malone Dev. Fed'n,* 13 F. Supp. 2d 101, 104 (C.D. Cal. 1998) (rejecting the doctrine of reverse equivalents), *aff'd,* 40 F.3d 16 (9th Cir. 1999).

- *Raymond v. Timmons,* 489 U.S. 16, 18 (1995) (citations omitted) (quoting *Jamison v. Woods,* 456 U.S. 890, 895 (1990)).

Exercise for Chapter 7

Correct the following statements and citations. There may be more than one thing wrong. Assume that state court cases are being cited in a memorandum.

1. In *Harris v. Baker,* 480 U.S. 620, 622–625 (1995) the Court held that fraud can consist of an "...omission just as much as an affirmative misrepresentation."

---

2. Indicate that the following Eighth Circuit case was an en banc decision that was later reversed by the U.S. Supreme Court the same year: *O'Hara v. Keyser,* 15 F.3d 18 (1997).

_____

3. In the following quotation, pluralize the word "director" and omit the words "to all shareholders": "A corporation may hold its board of director meeting in the state of incorporation or elsewhere so long as notice is given to all shareholders."

_____

_____

_____

4. "A restraint against alienation is invalid". *Sanders v. Maguire,* 901 F. Supp 18 (M.D. Pa. 1990), *Jacobs v. Farr,* 301 Cal. 650 (P. 2d 1999), *Peters v. Geoffrey Engineering Company,* 15 F.3d 96 (7th Circuit 1998), *Bailey v. Nelson,* 610 A. 2nd 106 (Maine 1990), and *Olson v. Olson,* 614 A. 2nd 909 (Maine 1993).

_____

_____

_____

5. "Judgments can always be . . . reduced". *Ivey v. Dolan,* 489 U.S. 674 (dissenting opinion by Associate Justice Kennedy) (original quotation appears in the middle of a sentence).

_____

_____

_____

6. Using appropriate parentheticals, indicate the following is a 9–0 decision that held that sole proprietors have unlimited personal liability: *Peck v. Hays,* 899 F.2d 240, 244–246 (Federal Circuit 1990), reversed at 422 U.S. 106 (1991).

_____

_____

_____

7. Show that you emphasized the phrase "duty bound to reveal" in the following quotation: "Concealment is the withholding of information that one is duty bound to reveal." *Simmons v. Friend Automobile Corporation,* 601 P.2d 14, 16 (Oklahoma 1995).

_____

_____

_____

8. The Court held that "malice must be proved for a plaintiff to recover punitive damages." *Bell v. Moore,* 510 U.S. 707, 714 (1997). Make the following changes: omit the phrase "for a plaintiff," emphasize the word "punitive," start your quote with the word "malice," and indicate that you omitted citations from your quote.

_____

_____

_____

CHAPTER 8 Short Forms, Signals, Related Authority, and Capitalization

SHORT FORMS (RULE 4; P.4)

Citation form is difficult and painstaking. Thus, any time you can avoid giving a citation in full, you should. In general, once a citation is given in full, you may later use a "short form" of it. The *Bluebook* states that short forms may be used if it will be clear to the reader what is being referenced, if the earlier full citation is in the same general discussion, and the reader can quickly locate the earlier full citation. Use of the short forms is optional, not mandatory. Do not give a short form until you have given the full citation.

Id. (Rule 4.1)

"*Id.*" is a signal meaning "in the same place" that instructs a reader to return to the immediately preceding citation, no matter what it is. Follow these four rules:

- The word *id.* is itself an abbreviation. Thus, it is always followed by a period.

- *Id.* is a foreign word. Thus, it should be italicized or underscored (when underscoring, underscore the period, as follows: <u>id.</u>).

- *Id.* can appear by itself, in which case it starts with a capital letter, or it can appear in the middle of a sentence, in which case it begins with a lowercase letter.

- The use of *id.* by itself tells the reader to go back to the immediately preceding authority. If you wish to send the reader to a different page, section, or paragraph within that authority, indicate that as shown in the following example.

Example:

The Court flatly announced its support for the doctrine of joint and several liability. *Farley v. Dayton-Hudson, Inc.,* 520 U.S. 16, 19 (1998). Thus, liability may be imposed upon any partner in a general partnership. *Id.* If, however, creditors know a partner has no authority to do a particular act, other partners may be insulated from liability. *Id.* at 26.

Three additional tips on using *id.* are:

- The use of *id.* for a case with a parallel citation does not significantly shorten the citation when you send the reader to a different page. For example, if the first citation is *Kenney v. Plaisance,* 231 Va. 16, 18, 204 S.E.2d 424, 427 (1990), the *id.* form is as follows: *Id.* at 21, 204 S.E.2d at 430. *Id.* only takes the place of the official citation.

- If citations are in footnotes rather than in the main body of the text, you cannot use *id.* to refer to an authority in a previous footnote if the footnote contains more than one citation (otherwise, the reader will not know to which of the preceding references the "*id.*" signals refers).

- Note that per Rule 3.4, you cannot use the word "at" before a section sign (§) or a paragraph symbol (¶).

Examples:

First reference (case page):	*Wilson v. Preston,* 490 U.S. 14, 16 (1995).
Second reference (case page):	*Id.* at 21.
Third reference (case page):	*Id.* at 24.
First reference (section sign):	Edward Riley, *Patent Practice* § 101 (1995).
Second reference (section sign):	*Id.* § 104. (Note: The word "at" is not used.)

Supra (Rule 4.2)

Supra means "above" and is a signal used to send a reader to a preceding citation, but not an immediately preceding citation. Note, however, that *supra* cannot be used to refer to primary authorities such as cases, statutes, or constitutions. It is thus used nearly exclusively to refer to previously cited books, law review and journal articles, and other secondary authorities. It must appear with the name of an author or some other identifying word rather than merely by itself, as does *id.* Although the *Bluebook* is clear that *supra* may not be used as a short form for cases or other primary authorities, many practitioners ignore this rule. Thus, do not be surprised to see the following: *Harrison Mfg., supra,* at 106.

Examples:

Page one of brief: Eve Jones, *Due Process,* 36 N.C. L. Rev. 401, 408 (1995).

Page two of brief: *Li v. Li,* 482 U.S. 120, 126 (1985).

Page three of brief: Jones, *supra.* or Jones, *supra,* at 412.

Note that in the preceding example, the use of *supra* directs the reader to the page within Eve Jones's article but does not tell the reader where exactly in your brief the reader will find your original citation to Eve Jones's article. Should you include this information? The *Bluebook* does not require that you tell the reader where in your document he or she will locate the previous citation but states you may do so (Rule 3.6). Use the following form: "Jones, *supra* p. 2, at 414" (directing the reader to page two of your document and then instructing the reader to review page 414 of Eve Jones's article). Note that "p." and "pp." are used only to direct a reader to pages within your document and not to pages within the published authority you are discussing.

When is *supra* followed by a comma? *Supra* is followed by a comma when you are directing the reader to the page or section of the previously cited published authority, as in "Jones, *supra,* at 414." When you are directing the reader to a previous page within your document—such as "Jones, *supra* p. 2, at 414."—there is no comma following the signal.

On rare occasions, a brief may use the signal *infra,* meaning "below," to send a reader to a citation given later. The rules governing *supra* apply equally to *infra*. It is more likely that you will encounter *infra* in indexes or texts. Thus, in Chapter 7 of a textbook you may be informed, "For a further discussion of this topic, see Chapter 10, *infra*." Similarly, authors use *infra* to send readers to a later section, as in "The issue of reckless conduct is discussed in Section IV, *infra*."

Use of "Hereinafter" (Rule 4.2(b))

Use "hereinafter" to abbreviate the name of a secondary authority that is long and cumbersome. Enclose the form in brackets. For example, use the following format: *Sonny Bono Copyright Term Extension Act: Hearings on S. 562 Before the House Comm. on Commerce*, 105th Cong. 121 (1997) [hereinafter *Copyright Hearings*]. Note two critical items: first, as with *supra* and *infra*, you cannot use "hereinafter" to refer to primary authorities (meaning you cannot use it as a shorthand signal for a case, statute, or constitution) and second, once you establish the shorthand abbreviation, you must consistently use it thereafter. Thus, any later reference to the preceding hearings must consistently be called *Copyright Hearings*. This later shortened reference will usually appear with *supra* as in the following: *Copyright Hearings, supra.*

Short Forms for Cases (Rule 10.9(a) and (b); P.4(a))

What if you cite a case on page two of your brief, then you cite a book on page three, and you wish to cite the case again on page four? You cannot use *id.* because that signal will send the reader to the book that is the immediately preceding citation. You cannot use *supra* because that signal cannot be used to send a reader to a case. Assume the case you cited on page one is *Li v. Li*, 482 U.S. 120, 126 (1985). There are three alternatives you may use.

- Option 1 (P.4(a)):   *Li*, 482 U.S. at 128.
- Option 2 (P.4(a)):   482 U.S. at 128.
- Option 3 (Rule 10.9(b)): Use "*Li*," with no further citation, if you have cited *Li* in the same general discussion, for example, "In *Li*, the Court also held . . . ."

You may choose the most appropriate option as long as the reader will have no doubt as to which case you are discussing. Thus, use options 2 and 3 only when you have been discussing the authority with such frequency that the reader will have no trouble locating the earlier citation. With regard to option 3, the *Bluebook* does not define the meaning of the term "same general discussion." Some authors view each section of a brief or memorandum as a separate discussion. A reference in a later-numbered section is thus not "in the same general discussion" and requires use of either option 1 or option 2. Use common sense, realizing that if you have not mentioned the *Li* case in several pages, the reader may have difficulty remembering or finding the citation if you only refer to it by name. In such instances, help the reader by giving more rather than less information.

Note: Although you should generally use the plaintiff's name when sending a reader back to a case, use the defendant's name if the plaintiff's name is a governmental or other common litigant such as "State" or "United States."

For cases with parallel citations, the short forms are not particularly short. For example, if your first citation was *Young v. Barwick,* 231 Va. 106, 108, 320 S.E.2d 114, 118 (1990), the later citation (assuming you cannot use *id.* because there is an intervening citation) is one of the following:

- *Young,* 231 Va. at 110, 320 S.E.2d at 120.

- 231 Va. at 110, 320 S.E.2d at 120.

- "In *Young,* the court also noted . . . ."

Short Forms for Other Authorities

Use the following short forms for authorities other than cases:

- For statutes and regulations, the first citation should be complete. Later references may use any form that clearly identifies the material (Rule 12.9). Thus, the first reference to a statute would be 17 U.S.C.A. § 101 (West 1998), while the later reference could be 17 U.S.C.A. § 101 or § 101 (Rule 12.9; P.4(b)).

- For constitutions, do not use any short form other than *id.* (Rule 11; P.4(c)).

- For books, law reviews, and other secondary authorities, use *id.* to send the reader to an immediately preceding authority and *supra* (with author's name or other identifying information) to send a reader to a source that is not immediately preceding, as in "McCarthy, *supra*, § 14.20." (Rule 4.2; P.4(d)).

Practice Tip:

✓ The words or abbreviations *id., supra,* and *infra* are always underscored or italicized, but "hereinafter" is not.

SIGNALS (RULE 1.2)

Introduction

Authorities cited by legal writers may support or contradict statements made by the writer or may merely provide background material. Citation signals allow a writer to indicate such without having to explain in full the specific manner in which the cited authority is used. Signals are thus a form of code, instantly conveying information to a reader. Unfortunately, cracking the code is difficult and uncertain due to the vague manner in which the *Bluebook* directs a writer as to the use of the signals.

Signals are divided into several categories: those that show support, those that suggest a useful comparison, those that indicate contradiction, and those that indicate background material. They precede case names or other authorities as follows: *See Brown v. Casey,* 500 U.S. 490, 495–98 (1998). If no signal is used before a citation, the reader should assume that the cited authority directly states the propostion, identifies the source of a quotation, or identifies the authority mentioned in text. The signal *see* indicates that the cited authority clearly supports the principle stated by the author. *See* is used instead of "no signal" when the propostion is not directly stated by the cited authority but obviously follows from it.

The situation is complicated by the fact that over the years, the use of certain signals has shifted. For example, until the Sixteenth Edition of the *Bluebook,* the use of no signal meant that the authority "clearly state[d]" the proposition discussed. According to the Sixteenth Edition, *see* was used to show that an authority "directly state[d]" a proposition. The Seventeenth Edition reverts to the position taken in the Fifteenth Edition, namely, that the use of no signal indicates that the cited authority directly states the proposition. Similarly, until the Sixteenth Edition, the signal *contra* informed a reader that the cited authority directly stated the contrary of the proposition. The signal *contra* did not exist in the Sixteenth Edition but reappeared in the Seventeenth Edition. Thus, analyzing briefs, documents, and articles written prior to late 2000 (when the Seventeenth Edition was issued) results in a different interpretation of some signals. (See Figure 8–1 for a chart showing changes in signals.)

What do these confusing rules and signals mean to practitioners? Consider the following tips:

- Review the signals set forth in Rule 1.2 and recognize that distinctions between some signals are nearly indecipherable.

- Use "no signal" when you are quoting or when the cited authority directly states the propostion.

- Use *see* when your authority clearly supports the statement you are making but requires an inferential step between the authority cited and the proposition it supports.

- When totally confused, consider using no signal and then discussing parenthetically the meaning of the authority cited, for example: *Parks v. Carter,* 432 P.2d 18, 20 (Cal. 1994) (holding that . . . .).

Presentation of Signals

Perhaps even more difficult than learning what the *Bluebook*'s signals mean is learning how to present the signals. Follow these guides:

- Capitalize the signal only if it begins a sentence. Otherwise, use a lowercase letter.

- Italicize or underscore signals when they are used in citation sentences or clauses (if the signal comprises two words, use a solid unbroken line, for example: See generally Paul S. Kaye, *Blue Sky Law,* 201 Mo. L. Rev. 118, 120 (1988)).

- When underscoring, separate the signal from an authority that is also underscored with a broken line, as follows: See Ford v. Hazard, 689 F.2d 118, 134 (9th Cir. 1990).

	Fifteenth Edition	**Sixteenth Edition**	**Seventeenth Edition**
[No signal]	Citation clearly states the proposition, identifies the source of a quotation, or identifies an authority referred to in text.	Citation identifies the source of a quotation or identifies an authority referred to in text.	Citation directly states the proposition, identifies the source of a quotation, or identifies an authority referred to in text.
See	Citation clearly supports the proposition.	Citation directly states or clearly supports the proposition.	Citation clearly supports the proposition.
Contra	Citation directly states the contrary of the proposition.	*Contra* signal did not exist in the Sixteenth Edition.	Citation directly states the contrary of the proposition.

Figure 8–1   Chart Showing Changes in *Bluebook* Signals

- When combining the signal *see* with another signal such as *e.g.* (to indicate that other authorities also state or support the proposition, but giving their citations would not be particularly helpful), follow the word *see* with a comma, as follows: *See, e.g., Allen v. Riley,* 610 P.2d 118 (Wyo. 1997).

- Do not italicize or underscore the signal if you use the signal as an ordinary verb in a sentence rather than as a shorthand instruction to the reader. Thus, the following is correct: For a general discussion of deeds of trust, see 78 C.J.S. *Deeds and Conveyances* § 48 (1994).

- When using a variety of signals within a "string," note that Rule 1.3 imposes a hierarchy on their presentation, meaning they should be listed in the order in which they are presented in the *Bluebook* (for example, supporting signals are listed before contradictory ones). If there are two supporting signals, they should be separated from each other by semicolons. If those two signals are followed by a signal indicating contradiction, a new sentence should be started to show the new type of signal.

- Authorities within each signal are separated by semicolons and presented in the order given in Rule 1.4 (statutes listed before cases, federal cases listed before state cases, cases from higher courts listed before cases from lower courts, and so forth).

Conclusion

The use of citation signals is frustrating even for the most practiced writers. Continually and carefully review their meanings. Reread Rule 1.2 several times so you can quickly and immediately convey to a reader the import of the authorities you cite. In the long run, mastering the citation signals will save you much time.

RELATED AUTHORITY (RULE 1.6; P.1(e))

On occasion, writers may wish to direct a reader to an authority related to or which discusses or quotes the specific authority cited. Such direction is accomplished through an italicized (or underscored) phrase that does not appear in parentheses. Commonly used directions include *quoted in, construed in, available at,* and *questioned in.* Use the following format: Hatch Act § 1, 36 U.S.C. § 50 (1996), *construed in James v. NRCC,* 520 U.S. 118, 126–27 (1997). If underscoring, use a solid unbroken line for the phrase, as follows: Linda Allen, <u>Treble Damages in Antitrust Cases</u>, 6 Duke L.J. 203 (1994), <u>reprinted in</u> Philip Hendrix, <u>The Law of Antitrust</u> (3d ed. 1999).

Note that a parenthetical explanation that follows an authority and whose first word ends with the suffix "ing" (such as "quoting," "citing," or "construing") is not italicized or underscored, although phrases that introduce related authority (such as *quoted in* or *reprinted in*) are underscored or italicized. Thus, the following is correct: *Monument Sav. Bank v. Tyson Fed'n,* 504 U.S. 106, 109 (1997) (quoting *Draper v. Farrell,* 501 U.S. 19, 22 (1995)).

CAPITALIZATION (RULE 8; P.6)

The *Bluebook* includes a number of rules relating to the capitalization of certain words. The most significant rules are as follows:

- Capitalize the "C" in Court:

  - ➤ Whenever you refer to the U.S. Supreme Court.

  - ➤ When referring to the court to which you are addressing a document or request (for example, always state "Plaintiff respectfully urges this Court to grant her Motion for Summary Judgment").

  - ➤ When identifying a specific court (as in the following: "The Eighth Circuit Court of Appeals clearly held that . . . .").

- Do not capitalize the "c" in "court" when you are discussing a court (other than the U.S. Supreme Court) in a general manner, such as follows: "The court in *Taylor* also held . . . .").

- Capitalize party identifications in the matter being adjudicated such as "Plaintiff," "Petitioner," or "Defendant," but not when they refer to parties in other actions, as follows: "The Defendant has asserted in his Answer that the action is barred by the statute of limitations. Plaintiff submits that Defendant has misinterpreted the position of the defendant in *Anderson.*"

- Capitalize the first letter in each significant word in the title of a court document, such as the following: "In Plaintiff's Motion to Compel Answers to Interrogatories, Plaintiff argues that . . . ."

- Capitalize proper nouns referring to the Constitution or various acts, such as "First Amendment," "Bill of Rights," and "Gold Clause Act."

- Capitalize "circuit" only when referring to a particular circuit, such as in the following statement: "The Ninth Circuit ruled that . . . ."

- Capitalize the "J" in justice or judge when giving the name of a specific jurist or when referring to any U.S. Supreme Court Justice, as in "Justice Roth" or "the Justice stated . . . ."

- Capitalize the word "state" when it is part of the full title of a state, as in "the State of Ohio."

Exercise for Chapter 8

A. Correct the following. Assume that each number to the left of a question refers to a page within a brief being submitted to a court in your state and that there are no intervening citations between questions. If alternate forms of citation are acceptable, give all. Assume the citations are "stand-alone" citations.

1. *Page v. Shaw,* 789 F.2d 113, 115, Ninth Circuit, 1990.

2. Refer to page 120 of the *Page* case.

3. Robertson, Patricia, *Employment Law,* § 13.01 (third edition 1990).

4. Refer to section 15.03 of Patricia Robertson's book.

5. Refer to page 125 of the *Page* case.

6. Refer to section 18.4 of Patricia Robertson's book.

B. Correct the following and describe the meaning of any signal used.

1. See generally *Poole v. Gammon,* 691 P. 2nd 14, 16 (Alaska 1990).

2. E.g. *Harrison v. Jacobs Publishing Company* 12 F. Supp. 2nd 181 (District, New Jersey 1998).

3. For additional discussion, see Frank Taylor, *Environmental Land Use,* 13 Natural Resources Journal 154, 156–159 (1997).

C. Correct the following statements made in a brief submitted to a court.

Although the defendant has repeatedly requested that the state of Minnesota provide him with copies of the police report, the State has failed to do so. Such a refusal is clearly a violation of the defendant's rights as guaranteed under the seventh amendment as well as under the Grayson act. As recently as June, the fourth circuit announced that such documents must be provided to all Litigants. Therefore, defendant respectfully urges this court to grant his motion to dismiss. As stated by justice Bronson, "only when documents are fully disclosed are a party's constitutional rights protected under the pertinent amendment."

CHAPTER 9 Putting It Together

THE TABLE OF AUTHORITIES

Many documents need (and court rules may require) a table of the authorities cited in the document. The table is presented at or near the beginning of the document or brief. A table of authorities lists each authority cited in a brief (whether in text or footnotes) together with a reference to the page or pages of the document on which each appears so that readers can readily locate a discussion of specific cases or other authorities. While the *Bluebook* gives hundreds of pages of information about isolated citations, it provides no direction whatsoever as to setting up a table of authorities. Thus, comply with court rules (if they exist) or your firm or company practices (if they exist). Failing any direction, consider the following:

- Although many word processing programs will automatically extract citations from your document and create a table of authorities, some individuals still prefer to use the "old-fashioned" approach: listing each authority on an index card and then "shuffling" them until they are in the right order.

- Citations that appear in a table of authorities are literally "standalone" citations (in that they appear by themselves rather than in a textual sentence), which would thus, per Table T.6 of the *Bluebook*, allow for abbreviation of words in a case name, such as "Bankruptcy," "Development," and "Society." Nevertheless, most practitioners prefer not to abbreviate such words in the table of authorities and only abbreviate widely known acronyms and the eight words listed in Rule 10.2.1(c), such as "Co." and "Corp.," so that the table, often the first substantive part of a brief reviewed by a reader, has a formal, complete, and professional appearance.

- If you decide to use full case names rather than treating the citations in the table as "stand-alones," as discussed previously, be especially careful when allowing a word processing program to create your table. If on page 6 of your brief, for example, you refer to "*Cooley Agric. Bd. v. Redmond Indem. Co.,* 15 F. Supp. 2d 18 (D.N.J. 1998)," a word processing program will recreate the citation in your table exactly in that form, requiring you to manually convert the citation to "*Cooley Agriculture Board v. Redmond Indemnity Co.,* 15 F. Supp. 2d 18 (D.N.J. 1998)" for the table of authorities.

- Group your citations together according to the type of authority. For example, list all the cases together under the heading "Cases," then all of the statutes under the heading "Statutes," then all of the miscellaneous authorities, and so forth. If your brief consists mainly of cases with only a few other authorities, your table will likely have just two categories: "Cases" and "Other Authorities." List primary authorities before you list secondary authorities. Remember that unless court rules require a certain organization, there are no rigid rules regarding preparation of tables of authorities. Consider the reader and use a presentation that readily communicates information. Some writers follow Rule 1.4 relating to the order of citations in strings as a guideline to the order of citations for a table of authorities.

- Within each grouping, list authorities alphabetically (listing cases alphabetically by plaintiff, such that the *Baker* case appears before the *Franklin* case which appears before *In re Carr* which appears before the *Jacobs* case); by ascending number (such that 15 U.S.C. § 2041 (1996) appears before 15 U.S.C. § 2049 (1996) which appears before 18 U.S.C. § 101 (1996)); or by author's name (such that an article by Thomas Howard is listed before one by Christopher Walter).

- Do not include introductory signals (such as *see*) or parenthetical expressions (such as "explaining that. . . .").

- Include subsequent history of a citation (such as *cert. denied* or *aff'd*) inasmuch as it is part of the full citation.

- Omit pinpoint citations in the table of authorities.

- Ensure that each time an authority is mentioned (whether in text or footnotes), the table reflects such. Thus, if your brief includes a reference to a certain case on page 4, and then there is an *id.* reference to the same case on page 5, and a later short form reference to the same case on page 11, the table should reflect that the case is discussed on pages 4, 5, and 11.

- Use *passim* rather than listing each page on which the authority appears if you cite a certain authority on numerous occasions throughout the document.

- Always double-check the table of authorities to ensure that if the table says a certain authority is discussed on pages 10 and 14 of your brief, it is discussed on those pages.

FOOTNOTES

Many legal writers prefer to cite their authorities in footnotes rather than in the narrative portion of the text. Other writers use both techniques in the same document, placing some authorities in the text of the document and others in footnotes. Endnotes (listing all authorities on a separate page at the end of a document) are rarely, if ever, used by legal writers.

There are two schools of thought on the use of footnotes. Some writers believe that using citations throughout the narrative is distracting and, thus, placing the citations in footnotes facilitates uninterrupted reading of a document. Other writers believe exactly the opposite, reasoning that when readers encounter a footnote either they train themselves to ignore it (in which case, the footnote is of no value) or, indulging a natural curiosity, they jump from the narrative to the footnote to see what it says, thus interrupting the flow of the argument.

Some courts have rules regarding or even prohibiting the citation of authorities in footnotes (realizing that typeface in footnotes is often smaller than that used in the narrative portion of text, thus allowing writers to squeeze more material into a brief and perhaps exceed page limits), and others limit the number of footnotes that may be used. Review these rules and consult with colleagues in your office to determine if one practice is more favored than another.

If citing authorities in footnotes, consider the following:

- Because footnotes in and of themselves can be distracting, do not distract readers further by appending excessive substantive explanatory parentheticals to cases cited. For example, avoid the following approach: "[1] *Dyer v. Maxwell,* 904 F.2d 118, 130–34 (9th Cir. 1994) (holding that abandonment of a trademark is presumed to have occurred after three years, although the presumption can be overcome by clear and convincing evidence otherwise, such as occurs when the trademark owner has made use of the mark customary in its trade or profession, so long as that use is not merely a token use)." If an issue merits substantive discussion, it likely merits discussion in the body of the work. Moreover, some readers have trained themselves to ignore footnotes, believing information therein is likely to be extraneous to the main argument. Thus, making arguments in footnotes may well be futile.

- Avoid footnotes that continue from one page to the next. For example, consider a reader who is reviewing page four of a brief and encounters a footnote. The reader glances down at the bottom of page four, begins reading the footnote, and must continue on to pages five and six to finish reading the footnote. When finished reading the footnote, the reader must return to page four and remember where he or she left off. Such a style is terribly distracting for almost all readers. Some will not return to the original page, thus missing significant portions of an analysis.

- If there are several citations within one footnote, the use of *id.* will send a reader to the immediately preceding authority within that same footnote. Alternatively, *id.* can be used as a footnote to refer to a preceding separate footnote, as long as there is only one authority cited within that preceding footnote.

- If you are directing a reader to a footnote within a source you cite, indicate as follows: "Harry S. Hunter, Annotation, *Tobacco Litigation,* 78 A.L.R.4th 106, 108 n.14 (1996)." (See Rule 3.3(b).) Note that there is no space between the "n." and the footnote reference. Cite multiple footnotes as follows: "nn.343–47."

INTERNAL CROSS-REFERENCES (RULE 3.6)

If you wish to send a reader to another part of the brief or document itself, be as specific as possible. Although there is nothing prohibiting you from merely directing the reader, "See Section III, *supra,*" it is easier for the reader if you provide the exact page, as follows: "See Section III, *supra* p. 8." This directs the reader to page 8 within your document to review Section III. Note that "p." and "pp." (for "pages") are used only for internal cross-references.

As discussed in Chapter 8, although the *Bluebook* does not require it, many authors prefer to tell readers where in the brief they can locate previously cited authorities. For example, if you cite a book by Charles Grant on page two of your brief, then you discuss and cite a variety of other authorities, and then on page six you again cite Charles Grant's book, you may do so as follows: "Grant, *supra* p. 2, at 909" (directing the reader to return to page two of your brief and then to review page 909 of Charles Grant's book).

If you are directing a reader to a previous footnote within your brief, follow the format: "Grant, *supra* note 23, at 909" (directing the reader to return to footnote number 23 in your brief and then to review page 909 of Charles Grant's book).

Remember that when directing a reader to pages or notes within your brief, *supra* is not followed by a comma (as in "Grant, *supra* note 23, at 909"). When directing a reader to a page within the previously cited authority, *supra* is followed by a comma (as in "Grant, *supra*, at 909").

Practice Tip:

✓ Because the addition or deletion of any material from your document will likely cause changes in pagination, insert the internal cross-reference page numbers only when the document is near completion. Use blank lines as you prepare the document, then replace them with actual page numbers just before final typing. Alternatively, you can use a unique combination of letters (perhaps your initials or XOX) instead of blank lines, then use the "find" and "replace" functions on your word processor to replace these initials with the actual page numbers.

FINAL TASKS IN CITE-CHECKING

Before any document that includes citations leaves your office, take the following last steps to ensure the document is errorless:

- Proofread carefully to ensure typists or word processors correctly made the revisions you requested.

- Be alert to inconsistency. If you underscored case names, then book titles and signals should be similarly underscored. Ensure that the document does not flip back and forth between underscoring and italicizing, which can easily occur if more than one author has worked on the document.

- Make sure the final document is printed by one printer because the use of different printers can result in a different appearance among pages.

- Recheck all of the short form signals, such as *id.* and *supra.* If material has either been added to or deleted from a document, these signals may well be incorrect.

- Check the accuracy of each quotation. Quotations must be reproduced scrupulously. If changes are made, make sure they are indicated through the use of ellipses or bracketed information.

- Check to make sure pinpoints are included for all citations.

- Review the table of authorities to ensure that all cases names are full and complete (with only commonly known acronyms and words such as "Inc." and "Corp." abbreviated) and that the references to the pages in the document on which authorities appear are correct. Do not rely exclusively on word processing programs to reproduce the table. Do your own proofreading.

Exercise for Chapter 9

Use a separate sheet of paper to create a table of authorities for the following. You may need to supply missing information and make corrections in the citations.

Eighth Ave. Financial Corp. v. Huntington Associates, 899 F. 2d 118 (Ninth Circuit 1999), cert. denied, 490 U.S. 116 (1999)

35 U.S.C.A. § 107

35 U.S.C.A. § 101

Franklin Park Comm. V. Baldwin Brothers, 12 F. Supp. 2d 18, 30 (Eastern District Texas 1998).

Bailey vs. Malone Central Insurance Company, 649 P.2d 18, 21 (Okl. 1990)

Brian Walsh, <u>Venue Practice</u> § 1.01 (4th edition 1990)

15 U.S.C.A. § 1051

Janet Holt, <u>Contract Administration</u>, 190, 195 (1994).

State v. Jackson Park, 651 P. 2d 409 (Okl. 1991)

28 U.S.C.A. §§ 201, 204, 206

Oklahoma Annotated Stat. Title 32 Section 414

In re Lowell, 355 U.S. 64, 68 (1980) (cited throughout the brief)

Stephanie Wallace, Annotation, *Regulation of Commerce on the Internet,* 101 A.L.R.4th 16, n. 4 (1995)

Hanley v. Woods, 490 U.S. 16, 24 (1998)

CHAPTER 10 The Final Review

Correct the citations in the following briefs and memorandum. For state court cases cited in the briefs, assume each is being cited in a brief being submitted to a court in that state. You may need to create missing information. Follow *Bluebook* rules.

BRIEF 1

Corporations are entities existing under the authority of a state legislature. Samuelson General Co v. Mutual Southern Inc. 201 United States 119, 121–123 (1990). Because corporations are viewed as persons in the eyes of the law, *Jacobs Machine Corp. v. Simpson Publishing Co.,* 15 F. 3rd 180 (Seventh Circuit 1994), they are thus subject to taxation. Samuelson, supra.

Generally, a corporation shields its shareholders from liability for debts and obligations. Cayton Organization Co. Inc. V. Social Technology Company, 242 Wisc. 2d 190 (1990); Francis v. Thompson Business Associates, 504 U.S. 116, 125–129 (1990); Gregory Chemical Plant Co v. Thomas J. Harris, Jr., 510 U.S. 16 (1991). Nevertheless, in certain situations, shareholders can be held liable for corporate obligations. Generally, if shareholders do not respect that the corporation is a separate entity, courts will act likewise. *Cayton, id.* This theory is generally referred to as "piercing the corporate veil." Jacob Taylor III, Corporate Law Treatise, § 14 (fifth edition 1995).

Courts have stated that they will pierce the veil whenever necessary to "prevent fraud or injustice". Corporate Law Treatise at § 16. Typically, however, what shareholders must show is either that shareholders are using the corporation as their alter ego or that the corporation was undercapitalized when it incurred its debts. Francis, supra. In fact, some state statutes have codified this principle. Delaware Code title 42, sections 119, et seq.

It is generally easier for a creditor to show that the corporation has been utilized as the shareholders' alter ego than to prove undercapitalization. Corporate Law Treatise at sections 142–148. As one court has stated:

> "The most common method of proving "alter ego" is to show either that the shareholders and the corporation have commingled their assets or that various corporate formalities have not been observed. Thus, the use of corporate funds by a shareholder to pay personal expenses may result in piercing of the veil. Similarly, failure of the corporation to observe basic corporate formalities such as holding meetings and elections may result in piercing of the veil." *Hays v. Anderson Advertising Co.*, 510 U.S. 10 (1997).

The majority shareholder of the defendant in this case has acknowledged that the corporation held only one meeting in the past three years. (Deposition of Shirley Hamilton, page 14). Similarly, the corporation has failed to hold any elections during that time period. "Elections of directors are an integral part of corporate existence. Failure to hold such elections *may well result* in "piercing of the veil" such that shareholders are liable to corporate creditors". Susan B. Kimball and Jean B. Higgins, 18 *Houston Law Review* 130, 146 (emphasis in original). Other acts of neglect of the corporation can also be considered by courts in determining whether the corporate veil of limited liability can or should be pierced. *Hays* at 23.

Because the evidence clearly establishes in this case that the defendant corporation and defendants Carol Yost and Joseph Yost have failed to observe even the most basic of corporate formalities, they should be denied the protection of corporate existence and be held liable for the corporation's obligations.

Pursuant to Federal Rule of Civil Procedure 53 (a), plaintiff thus urges this court to grant his motion to strike affirmative defenses.

BRIEF 2

In the present case, the plaintiff has argued that defendant Anderson Herald Publishing Co. (hereinafter "Anderson") has abandoned its trademark through failure to use the mark. Defendant will show that such is not the case.

Trademarks are acquired through use. 15 U.S.C. §1501. Similarly, rights to trademarks can be lost through nonuse. 15 U.S.C. § 1554. Abandonment of a trademark, however, is a serious loss and thus courts have typically refused to order that a mark has been abandoned unless there is clear and convincing evidence of such. Hyatt v. Marshall Automobile Co., 12 F. Supp (Second) 101 (District of Columbia 1995). In Hyatt, the Court held that a press conference announcing that the company had selected a new mark to reflect its new corporate image and would cease use of the existing mark showed "... a manifest intent to abandon the mark."

Other acts can also be used to support a finding of voluntary abandonment. For example, licensing the mark to another and failing to impose any requirements on the licensee's use of the mark is inconsistent with the owner's duty to monitor and protect its mark. Matthew J. Fletcher, III, *Trademark Use and Policing*, 54 A.L.R. (4th) 118 (1996).

In fact, such an agreement is often called a "naked license" and may result in absolute loss of the mark to the licensee. Id. at 142–144. Once lost, such a mark cannot be reacquired. Hyatt, supra.

Loss of trademark rights can also result from an extended period of nonuse. In fact, nonuse of a mark for three years creates a presumption that it has been abandoned. 15 U.S.C.A §§ 1059–61. Although the presumption is rebuttable, *Hyatt,* the evidence required to overcome the presumption must be compelling.

For example, it is possible that nonuse may be excusable. Courts have found that failure to use a mark because of transportation strikes preventing shipping, labor unrest, and acts of God may justify nonuse of a mark. Fletcher at 121. Nevertheless, failure to use a mark because of economic conditions rarely, if ever, justifies nonuse. Gregory and Ellen Nelson vs. Construction Distributing Co., 989 F. 2nd 121 (1994), affirmed at 488 U.S. 16 (1995).

If an owner of a mark loses rights to the mark due to abandonment through nonuse and a third party begins using the mark, the owner cannot recreate rights in the mark through subsequent use. Baker v. Carey, 501 U.S. 116 (1998); 72 C.J.S. *Trademarks,* Section 72; Talbott Housing Co. vs. Mayfair Hills Inc., 901 F.2d 14, 16 (8th Circuit 1998), cert. denied 500 U.S. 28 (1998). The original owner's rights, if any, stem from the date of its subsequent use. If such use is after that of the intervening third party, the third party has superior rights to the mark. *Nelson* at 124.

Finally, a mere token use of a mark will not serve to defeat a presumption of nonuse. J. Thomas McCarthy, *McCarthy on Trademarks and Unfair Competition,* § 4.42 (volume 3, 4th Ed. 1995). Thus, merely using the mark one time or using it in internal communications rather than for bona fide sales will not suffice. Id. at § 4.47.

In the present case, defendant's records show that use of the mark in question has been, at best, a token use. (Affidavit of Hunter Tracht, Paragraph 16). Such use will not serve to overcome the presumption that defendant's failure to use the mark for four years is an abandonment of the mark within the meaning of *Hyatt.*

Thus, plaintiff thus urges this court to grant its motion for summary judgment.

MEMORANDUM

To: Allen Amey
From: Susan Davis
Re: Claim of Sexual Harassment by Linda Denman
Date: September 30

Factual Background

Our client, Linda Denman ("Denman") is employed by Tech Solutions Integrators, Inc. ("TSI"). During the past six months, Denman, who is the only female on her project team, has noticed that the males on her team have engaged in sexually suggestive jokes and comments using crude language. Denman has been present during these conversations and has, on occasion, traded sexually suggestive quips with others on the team. Last week, one of the employees used his work desk computer to retrieve photographs of naked women from the Internet. The computer was placed so that any employee who walked by the desk could readily see the screen. Linda walked by, saw the photographs, and has inquired whether she may file a lawsuit against Tech Solutions alleging sexual harassment in the workplace.

Analysis

<u>Section I: Introductory Principles.</u> Sexual harassment is prosecuted as sexual discrimination under the Civil Rights Act of 1964. 42 USCS § § 2000e et seq. While the language of the statute does not specifically address sexual harassment, case law has interpreted the statute to mean that sexual harassment is actionable as discrimination based on

sex. Sara T. Garner, L.L.B., Annotation, When the Workplace is Hostile 76 ALR Fed 158, 260-266. The Supreme Court, in Evans v. Merriman Guar. Sav. Bank, 478 US 67 (1987), citing federal employment regulation 29 CFR § 1603.21 (a) found that two types of sexual harassment are actionable under the Act: harassment that conditions tangible employment benefits on sexual favors (referred to as "quid pro quo" harassment) and harassment that, while not affecting economic benefits, creates a hostile or offensive working environment ("hostile work environment" harassment). Because there is no evidence of quid pro quo harassment of Linda at TSI, any claim would be based on the hostile work environment at TSI.

The issue of Denman's participation in the conduct complained of will be discussed in Section II, infra.

In Merriman, U.S. at 81, the court relied on Green v. E.E.O.C., 681 F. 2d 897 (3rd Circuit Ct. of App. 1985), affirmed at 470 U.S. 904 (1986), for the standards required to find conduction actionable as "hostile work environment" harassment. The court stated that the conduct must be so

"severe or pervasive that it altered the conditions of ... employment."

The next year, the Court reiterated its decision in Merriman, adding that to determine whether a hostile environment had been created the lower Courts should consider all of the circumstances set forth in 29 CFR §1603.21, such as the frequency of the conduct, whether the conduct was threatening or humiliating, and if the conduct interfered with the Plaintiff's work performance. Grayson v. Fording Systems Inc., 509 US 27, 33, reh. denied, 510 US 189 (1987).

Under these standards, sexual harassment need not be limited to unwanted physical contact, but can also include the display of obscene pictures. *Harrington v. Frederick Metropolitan Reproduction and Photo Co.,* 951 F.Supp. 403, 411 (C.D. Calif. 1996) (photography company employee had a reasonable belief that an assignment to work on a sexually explicit photograph could constitute sexual harassment). However, in *Harding v. Harmony Found.,* 13 F. 3rd 1004 (Eighth Circuit 1996), certiorari denied, 500 US 16 (1996), the court found that isolated incidents not directed specifically toward a Plaintiff are merely offensive and not actionable as harassment. Relying upon Foster vs. Federal Aviation Administration, 776 F. Supp. 403 (Ark. 1992), the Court in Harding stated that the conduct must be persistent to be actionable.

In *Grayson,* the supreme court applied a two-pronged standard in determining whether conduct is actionable: an objective standard from a reasonable person's view and a subjective standard whether the claimant perceives the work environment to be abusive. Several state courts have stated that the objective standard is satisfied when the Defendant creates an offensive environment and adversely affects the Plaintiff's working conditions, as would be perceived by a reasonable person. <u>Fuller v. Board of Education of Oakland, California</u>, 689 P. 2d 91 (Cal. 1996). The Defendant's conduct need not be intended as harassment and the adverse effect need not be pervasive. Id. Nor must the plaintiff prove a decline in tangible productivity. Garner, supra.

Denman's case satisfies these standards. In Otto v. Park Dev. Co., 699 P. 2d 18, 21–26 (Cal. 1997), the Court found that a single incident of leaving an adult magazine on the plaintiff's desk combined with gender-related harassment met the court's minimal *prima facie* standards of sexual harassment. Similarly, in the present case, if Denman's work environment was adversely affected due to the creation of a hostile working environment by Tech Solutions, the objective standard for proving sexual harassment has been satisfied.

Answer Keys

EXERCISE FOR CHAPTER 2

The following are examples found in the *Bluebook*. Correct them for use by practitioners.

1. RESTATEMENT (THIRD) OF UNFAIR COMPETITION § 3 (1985).

   Restatement (Third) of Unfair Competition § 3 (1985).

2. U.S. CONST. art. 1, § 9, cl. 2.

   U.S. Const. art. 1, § 9, cl. 2.

3. CAL. VEH. CODE § 11,509 (West 1987 & Supp. 1991).

   Cal. Veh. Code § 11,509 (West 1987 & Supp. 1991).

4. 17 AM. JUR. 2d *Contracts* § 74 (1964).

   17 Am. Jur. 2d *Contracts* § 74 (1964).

5. Kim Lane Scheppele, *Foreword: Telling Stories*, 87 MICH. L. REV. 2073, 2082 (1989).

   Kim Lane Scheppele, *Foreword: Telling Stories*, 87 Mich. L. Rev. 2073, 2082 (1989).

6. S. REP. NO. 89–910, at 4 (1965).

   S. Rep. No. 89–910, at 4 (1965).

EXERCISE FOR CHAPTER 3

Correct the following citations. You may need to supply or create missing information. There may be more than one thing wrong with the citation. (Note: Case names and signals may be either underscored or italicized.)

Case Names

1. John Oliver versus T.J. Younger

    Oliver v. Younger

2. H.L. Keane, Jr. Vs. Susan Jones, Ann Edwards, and Raymond Harris

    Keane v. Jones

3. State of Minnesota V. Baker Automobile Corporation (Assume citation appears as a "stand-alone" and is a Minnesota case.)

    State v. Baker Auto. Corp.

4. USA v. Franklin Liability Indemnity Company (Cite first assuming citation appears in a textual sentence, and then cite as a stand-alone citation.)

    United States v. Franklin Liability Indemnity Co.

    United States v. Franklin Liab. Indem. Co.

5. Jacob and Pamela Iverson versus Central Intelligence Agency

    Iverson v. CIA
          or
    Iverson v. Central Intelligence Agency

State Court Cases

6. Gray v. Gray, 692 Michigan 16. (Assume citation appears in a brief submitted to a Michigan court.)

    Gray v. Gray, 692 Mich. 16, xxx N.W. xxx (19xx).

7. Bradley v. Browning, 201 Cal. 2d 192, 78 California Reporter 14, 451 Pacific Reporter (Second Series) 16 (1998). (Assume citation appears in a brief submitted to a California court.)

    Bradley v. Browning, 201 Cal. 2d 192, 451 P.2d 16, 78 Cal. Rptr. 14 (1998).

8. Bradley v. Browning, 201 Cal. 2d 192, 78 California Reporter 14, 451 Pacific Reporter (Second Series) 16, 1998. (Assume citation appears in a letter to an adversary.)

   Bradley v. Browning, 451 P.2d 16 (Cal. 1998).

9. Walters v. Barry Redmond, an Oklahoma case decided in 1990.

   Walters v. Redmond, xxx P.2d xxx (Okla. 1990).

   (Note: Because Oklahoma stopped publishing officially in 1953, all cases since 1953 are found only in P. or P.2d.)

Federal Cases and Subsequent History

10. Bennett v. Bianco, 429 United States 16, 201 Supreme Court Reporter 12, 309 Lawyers' Edition, Second, 436 (1990).

    Bennett v. Bianco, 429 U.S. 16 (1990).

11. Farley v. State of Arizona, a 2000 Third Circuit case located in volume 401 of the Federal Reporter (Third Series) at page 19. (Assume *certiorari* was granted for this case by the Supreme Court in 2000).

    Farley v. State, 41 F.3d 19 (3d Cir.), *cert. granted,* xxx U.S. xxx (2000).

12. Hawken vs. Smith, 12 F. 3d 28 (1996). (Assume this case was reversed by the United States Supreme Court in 1997.)

    Hawken v. Smith, 12 F.3d 28 (___ Cir. 1996), *rev'd,* xxx U.S. xxx (1997).

    (Note: Answer must include some reference to a circuit court of appeals.)

13. Sanchez v. Barclay Bank of Miami, Florida, (1995) 903 Federal Supplement 892.

    Sanchez v. Barclay Bank, 903 F. Supp. 892 (M.D. Fla. 1995).

    (Note: Other district court abbreviations are acceptable.)

14. Powell v. Silvers, a case from the Eastern District of Virginia, decided in 1998 and affirmed by the Fourth Circuit Court of Appeals in 1999.

Powell v. Silvers, xxx F. Supp. 2d xxx (E.D. Va. 1998), *aff'd,* xxx F.3d xxx (4th Cir. 1999).

(Note: F. Supp. may also be acceptable.)

Spacing

15. 13 Federal Reporter (Third Series) 892 (1996).

    13 F.3d 892 (1996).

16. 391 California Appellate Reports, Third Series, page 109 (1984).

    391 Cal. App. 3d 109 (1984).

17. Ellis v. Ellis, 390 United States Reports 90 (1985).

    Ellis v. Ellis, 390 U.S. 90 (1985).

18. Sands v. Victor, 201 N. C. 14, 301 S. E. 2nd 19 (1989).

    Sands v. Victor, 201 N.C. 14, 301 S.E.2d 19 (1989).

19. 36 Boston College Law Review 19 (1990).

    36 B.C. L. Rev. 19 (1990).

20. 45 New York University Law Review 144 (1982).

    45 N.Y.U. L. Rev. 144 (1982).

EXERCISE FOR CHAPTER 4

Correct the following citations. You may need to supply missing information.

1. Fifth Amendment to the U.S. Constitution.

   U.S. Const. amend. V.

2. Article 2, Section 1, clause 4, of the U.S. Constitution.

   U.S. Const., art. II, § 1, cl. 4.

3. Article V of the New Mexico Constitution.

   N.M. Const. art. V.

4. House of Representatives bill number 1209, 106th Congress.

H.R. 1209, 106th Cong. § x (19xx).

or

H.R. 1209, 106th Cong. (19xx).

5. Statement of Senator Dole, volume 139 of the Congressional Record, at page 190.

139 Cong. Rec. 190 (19xx) (statement of Sen. Dole).

6. Judicial Nominations: Hearing on Senate Bill No. 901 before the Senate Judiciary Committee, held during the 105th Congress, Statement of Lawrence V. McConnell, Judge, Central District of California.

Judicial Nominations: Hearing on S. 901 Before the Senate Comm. on the Judiciary, 105th Cong. xx (19xx) (statement of Lawrence V. McConnell, Judge, C.D. Cal.).

7. Title 11, Section 311 of the United States Code.

11 U.S.C. § 311 (19xx).

8. Section 981 of Title 35 of United States Code Annotated. (Assume the statute is found in the pocket part.)

35 U.S.C.A. § 981 (West Supp. 19xx).

9. 42 United States Code Service Sections 303 to 307 (1996).

42 U.S.C.S. §§ 303-307 (Law. Co-op. 1996).

10. Idaho Code Sections 30-1-1 to 30-1-14.

Idaho Code §§ 30-1-1 to 30-1-14 (Michie 19xx).

(Note: Rule 3.4(b) provides that if using a hyphen or dash would be ambiguous, one should use the word "to.")

11. Delaware Code, title 8, section 155.

Del. Code Ann. tit. 8, § 155 (19xx).

12. Maryland Code, Corporations and Associations, Sections 3-700 to 3-709.

Md. Code Ann., Corps. & Ass'ns §§ 3-700 to 3-709 (19xx).

13. California Streets and Highways Section 1440.

   Cal. Sts. & High. § 1440 (West 19xx).
   or
   Cal. Sts. & High. § 1440 (Deering 19xx).

14. Uniform Commercial Code Section 2-201.

   U.C.C. § 2-201 (19xx).

15. Federal Rule of Civil Procedure 53 (a).

   Fed. R. Civ. P. 53(a).

16. House of Representatives Report Number 106-09, page 24.

   H.R. Rep. No. 106-09, at 24 (19xx).

EXERCISE FOR CHAPTER 5

Correct the following citations. You may need to supply missing information.

1. The definition of "negligence" appearing on page 609 of Black's Law Dictionary.

   Black's Law Dictionary 609 (7th ed. 1999).

2. Volume 2 of the third edition of a book written by Gary Richards, entitled "Copyright and Computers," Sections 16 through 18.

   2 Gary Richards, *Copyright and Computers* §§ 16-18 (3d ed. 19xx).

3. A law review article appearing at page 106 of volume 101 of the Yale Law Journal, entitled "Racial Profiling" and written by Laura Harris.

   Laura Harris, *Racial Profiling,* 101 Yale L.J. 106 (19xx).

4. A discussion of Section 14 of the topic False Imprisonment in American Jurisprudence, Second Series, volume 12.

   12 Am. Jur. 2d *False Imprisonment* § 14 (19xx).

5. Section 46, comment c, of the Restatement of Trusts, Second.

   Restatement (Second) of Trusts § 46 cmt. c (19xx).

   (Note: See Rule 3.5 for citations to comments.)

6. A 1998 book written by Andrew Wilcox and Phillip Wilcox entitled "Law and Technology," Section 13.

   Andrew Wilcox & Phillip Wilcox, *Law and Technology* § 13 (1998).

7. A law review article published in the New Mexico Law Review in 1996, entitled "Navajo Tribal Council Law" and written by John W. Black, III.

   John W. Black, III, *Navajo Tribal Council Law*, xxx N.M. L. Rev. xxx (1996).

8. An annotation entitled "Ocean and Coastal Law" appearing in A.L.R. 5th in 1998 and written by Susan Lloyd Kaye.

   Susan Lloyd Kaye, Annotation, *Ocean and Coastal Law*, xxx A.L.R.5th xxx (1998).

9. Restatement of Contracts, Second Series, Section 97.

   Restatement (Second) of Contracts § 97 (19xx).

10. A September 1995 article written in the Justice System Journal at page 8 by James Raymond, entitled "Tort Reform: The Legislative Experience."

    James Raymond, *Tort Reform: The Legislative Experience*, Just. Sys. J. Sept., 1995, at 8.

    (Note: Rule 16.4 governs citation form for works appearing within periodicals that are separately paginated within each issue.)

EXERCISE FOR CHAPTER 6

Correct each citation. You may need to supply or create missing information. Assume citations are "stand-alone" citations.

1. Plaintiff's Deposition, page 42

   Pl.'s Dep. at 42

   Defendant's Answer to Interrogatory, page 14

   Def.'s Answer to Interrog. at 14
   or
   Def.'s Answer Interrog. at 14

Exhibit A

Ex. A

Plaintiffs' Points and Authorities, Paragraph 14

Pls.' P. & A. ¶ 14

Defendants' Counterclaim, Paragraph 16

Defs.' Countercl. ¶ 16

2. *Ott v. Park Development Co.*, volume 6, Labor Law Reports, Paragraph 1201.

Ott v. Park Dev. Co., 6 Lab. L. Rep. (CCH) ¶ 1201 (include court information and exact date).

3. Presidential Proclamation Number 5089. (Assume material is available in C.F.R.)

Proclamation No. 5089, 3 C.F.R. xxx (19xx).

4. Executive Order 16,019. (Assume material is available in C.F.R.)

Exec. Order No. 16,019, 3 C.F.R. xxx (19xx).

or

Exec. Order No. 16,019, 3 C.F.R. xxx (19xx), *reprinted in* 3 U.S.C. § xxx (19xx).

5. Section 121.101 of title 29 of *Code of Federal Regulations.*

29 C.F.R. § 121.101 (19xx).

6. *Brady v. Sanders,* No. 95-145, (11th Circuit May 9, 1996) LEXIS 907, U.S. App. 1996.

Brady v. Sanders, No. 95-145, 1996 U.S. App. LEXIS 907, at *x (11th Cir. May 9, 1996).

7. Article by Person, Candace E., entitled "Citation of Legal and Nonlegal Electronic Database Information" (last visited August 6, 1998) and located only at "http://www.michbar.org/publications/citation.htm."

Candace E. Person, *Citation of Legal and Nonlegal Electronic Database Information* (last visited Aug. 6, 1998), *at* http://www.michbar.org/publications/citation.htm.

8. "Priority Watch List Determinations," volume 68 of *Federal Register,*
    page 1901, to be codified in title 33 of *Code of Federal Regulations*
    at part 200.

    > Priority Watch List Determinations, 68 Fed. Reg. 1901 (exact
    > date) (to be codified at 33 C.F.R. pt. 200).

9. Give public domain citations for the following:

    a. *Parker v. Bonette Agency Service, Co.,* the 201st case in 1999 from
        the Sixth Circuit. (Use *Bluebook* format.)

        > *Parker v. Bonette Agency Serv., Co.,* 1999 FED App. 201 (6th
        > Cir.).

    b. *Talbot v. Taylor,* the 69th case in 1998 from the South Dakota
        Supreme Court, Paragraph 4 (also located at volume 505 of
        North Western Reporter, Second Series, at page 18).

        > *Talbot v. Taylor,* 1998 SD 69, ¶ 4, 505 N.W.2d 18, xx.

EXERCISE FOR CHAPTER 7

Correct the following statements and citations. There may be more
than one thing wrong. Assume that state court cases are being cited in
a memorandum.

1. In *Harris v. Baker,* 480 U.S. 620, 622–625 (1995) the Court held that
    fraud can consist of an ". . . omission just as much as an affirmative
    misrepresentation."

    > In *Harris v. Baker,* 480 U.S. 620, 622–25 (1995), the Court held that
    > fraud can consist of an "omission just as much as an affirmative
    > misrepresentation."

2. Indicate that the following Eighth Circuit case was an en banc deci-
    sion that was later reversed by the U.S. Supreme Court the same
    year: *O'Hara v. Keyser,* 15 F.3d 18 (1997).

    > *O'Hara v. Keyser,* 15 F.3d 18 (8th Cir.) (en banc), *rev'd,* xxx U.S. xxx
    > (1997).

3. In the following quotation, pluralize the word "director" and omit
    the words "to all shareholders": "A corporation may hold its board

of director meeting in the state of incorporation or elsewhere so long as notice is given to all shareholders."

"A corporation may hold its board of director[s] meeting in the state of incorporation or elsewhere so long as notice is given . . . ."

4. "A restraint against alienation is invalid". *Sanders v. Maguire*, 901 F. Supp. 18 (M.D. Pa. 1990), *Jacobs v. Farr*, 301 Cal. 650 (P. 2d 1999), *Peters v. Geoffrey Engineering Company*, 15 F.3d 96 (7th Circuit 1998), *Bailey v. Nelson*, 610 A. 2nd 106 (Maine 1990), and *Olson v. Olson*, 614 A. 2nd 909 (Maine 1993).

"A restraint against alienation is invalid." *Sanders v. Maguire*, 901 F. Supp. 18 (M.D. Pa. 1990); *Peters v. Geoffrey Eng'g Co.*, 15 F.3d 96 (7th Cir. 1998); *Jacobs v. Farr*, xxx P.2d xxx (Cal. 1999); *Olson v. Olson*, 614 A.2d 909 (Me. 1993); *Bailey v. Nelson*, 610 A.2d 106 (Me. 1990).

(Note: It is presumed the first citation is the most important and thus it is placed first, even though in this string, the first citation is from the lowest of the federal courts, one of the district courts.)

(Note: Although Maine has now adopted a public domain citation format, the format did not exist prior to December 31, 1996.)

5. "Judgments can always be . . . reduced". *Ivey v. Dolan*, 489 U.S. 674 (dissenting opinion by Associate Justice Kennedy) (original quotation appears in the middle of a sentence).

"[J]udgments can always be . . . reduced." *Ivey v. Dolan*, 489 U.S. 674, xxx (Kennedy, J., dissenting).

6. Using appropriate parentheticals, indicate the following is a 9–0 decision that held that sole proprietors have unlimited personal liability: *Peck v. Hays*, 899 F.2d 240, 244–246 (Federal Circuit 1990), reversed at 422 U.S. 106 (1991).

Peck v. Hays, 899 F.2d 240, 244–46 (Fed. Cir. 1990) (9–0 decision) (holding that sole proprietors have unlimited personal liability), *rev'd*, 422 U.S. 106 (1991).

7. Show that you emphasized the phrase "duty bound to reveal" in the following quotation: "Concealment is the withholding of information that one is duty bound to reveal." *Simmons v. Friend Automobile Corporation*, 601 P.2d 14, 16 (Oklahoma 1995).

"Concealment is the withholding of information that one is *duty bound to reveal.*" *Simmons v. Friend Auto. Corp.*, 601 P.2d 14, 16 (Okla. 1995) (emphasis added).

8. The Court held that "malice must be proved for a plaintiff to recover punitive damages." *Bell v. Moore*, 510 U.S. 707, 714 (1997). Make the following changes: omit the phrase "for a plaintiff," emphasize the word "punitive," start your quote with the word "malice," and indicate that you omitted citations from your quote.

"[M]alice must be proved . . . to recover *punitive* damages." *Bell v. Moore*, 510 U.S. 707, 714 (1997) (citations omitted) (emphasis added).

(Note: Rule 5.3 states that the parenthetical "(citation omitted)" is placed immediately after the citation.)

EXERCISE FOR CHAPTER 8

A. Correct the following. Assume that each number to the left of a question refers to a page within a brief being submitted to a court in your state and that there are no intervening citations between questions. If alternate forms of citation are acceptable, give all. Assume the citations are "stand-alone" citations.

1. *Page v. Shaw*, 789 F.2d 113, 115, Ninth Circuit, 1990.

   Page v. Shaw, 789 F.2d 113, 115 (9th Cir. 1990).

2. Refer to page 120 of the *Page* case.

   Id. at 120.

3. Robertson, Patricia, *Employment Law*, § 13.01 (third edition 1990).

   Patricia Robertson, *Employment Law* § 13.01 (3d ed. 1990).

4. Refer to section 15.03 of Patricia Robertson's book.

   Id. § 15.03.

5. Refer to page 125 of the *Page* case.

Page, 789 F.2d at 125.
or
789 F.2d at 125.
or
In *Page,* the court also held . . . . (assuming *Page* was discussed in the same general discussion)

6. Refer to section 18.4 of Patricia Robertson's book.

Robertson, *supra,* § 18.4.

B. Correct the following and describe the meaning of any signal used.

1. See generally *Poole v. Gammon,* 691 P. 2nd 14, 16 (Alaska 1990).

See generally Poole v. Gammon, 691 P.2d 14, 16 (Alaska 1990) (holding that . . . .).

The signal *see generally* indicates that the case provides helpful background information.

(Note: When underscoring, there should be a solid unbroken line for *see generally.* Pursuant to Rules 1.2(d) and 1.5, the use of an explanatory parenthetical is encouraged with a signal such as *see generally.* Thus, a parenthetical beginning with an expression such as "holding that" or "explaining that" is preferred.)

2. E.g. *Harrison v. Jacobs Publishing Company* 12 F. Supp. 2nd 181 (District, New Jersey 1998).

E.g., Harrison v. Jacobs Publ'g Co., 12 F. Supp. 2d 181 (D.N.J. 1998).

The signal *e.g.* indicates that the cited authority states the propostion. Other authorities also state the propostition, but citation to them would not be helpful or is not necessary.

3. For additional discussion, see Frank Taylor, *Environmental Land Use,* 13 Natural Resources Journal 154, 156–159 (1997).

For additional discussion, see Frank Taylor, *Environmental Land Use,* 13 Nat. Resources J. 154, 156–59 (1997).

In this example, "see" is used as a verb, and thus, it is neither underscored nor italicized.

C. Correct the following statements made in a brief submitted to a court.

Although the Defendant has repeatedly requested that the State of Minnesota provide him with copies of the police report, the state has failed to do so. Such a refusal is clearly a violation of the Defendant's rights as guaranteed under the Seventh Amendment as well as under the Grayson Act. As recently as June, the Fourth Circuit announced that such documents must be provided to all litigants. Therefore, Defendant respectfully urges this Court to grant his Motion to Dismiss. As stated by Justice Bronson, "only when documents are fully disclosed are a party's constitutional rights protected under the pertinent amendment."

EXERCISE FOR CHAPTER 9

Create a table of authorities for the following. You may need to supply missing information and make corrections in the citations.

TABLE OF AUTHORITIES

<u>Cases</u>   <u>Pages</u>

Bailey v. Malone Central Insurance Co., 649 P.2d 18
(Okla. 1990) 2, 4

Eighth Avenue Financial Corp. v. Huntingdon Associates, 899
F.2d 118 (9th Cir.), *cert. denied*, 490 U.S. 116 (1999) 16

Franklin Park Committee v. Baldwin Bros., 12 F. Supp. 2d 18
(E.D. Tex. 1998) 6, 12, 14

Hanley v. Woods, 490 U.S. 16 (1998) 12, 13

In re Lowell, 355 U.S. 64 (1980) . . . . *passim*

State v. Jackson Park, 651 P.2d 409 (Okla. 1991) 3, 13, 14

<u>Statutes</u>

15 U.S.C.A. § 1051 (West 19xx) 5

28 U.S.C.A. § 201 (West 19xx) 5, 7

28 U.S.C.A. § 204 (West 19xx) 5, 6

28 U.S.C.A. § 206 (West 19xx) 6, 7, 8

(Note: page numbers are fictitious and are provided merely for the user's convenience.)

CHAPTER 10 THE FINAL REVIEW

Correct the citations in the following briefs and memorandum. For state court cases cited in the briefs, assume each is being cited in a brief being submitted to a court in that state. You may need to create missing information. Follow *Bluebook* rules.

Note the following as you make your corrections:

• Underscoring rather than italicizing is acceptable (as long as it is done consistently throughout a document).

• Pinpoint citations have been added inasmuch as they are recommended and are customary.

• Pinpoints and other unknown information, such as dates, are indicated through the use of the symbol "xx" or "xxx".

• Note that periods and commas must appear inside quotation marks.

BRIEF 1

Corporations are entities existing under the authority of a state legislature. *Samuelson Gen. Co. v. Mut. S. Inc.,* 201 U.S. 119, 121–23 (1990). Because corporations are viewed as persons in the eyes of the law, *Jacobs Machine Corp. v. Simpson Publishing Co.,* 15 F.3d 180, xxx (7th Cir. 1994), they are thus subject to taxation. *Samuelson,* 201 U.S. at xxx [or just 201 U.S. at xxx].

Generally, a corporation shields its shareholders from liability for debts and obligations. *Cayton Org. Co. v. Soc. Tech. Co.*, 242 Wis. 2d 190, xxx, xxx N.W.2d xxx, xxx (1990); *Gregory Chem. Plant Co. v. Harris*, 510 U.S. 16, 19 (1991); *Francis v. Thompson Bus. Assoc.*, 504 U.S. 116, 125–29 (1990). Nevertheless, in certain situations, shareholders can be held liable for corporate obligations. Generally, if shareholders do not respect that the corporation is a separate entity, courts will act likewise. *Cayton*, 242 Wis. 2d at xxx, xxx N.W.2d at xxx [or just 242 Wis. 2d at xxx, xxx N.W.2d at xxx]. This theory is generally referred to as "piercing the corporate veil." Jacob Taylor III, *Corporate Law Treatise* § 14 (5th ed. 1995).

Courts have stated that they will pierce the veil whenever necessary to "prevent fraud or injustice." *Id.* § 16. Typically, however, what shareholders must show is either that shareholders are using the corporation as their alter ego or that the corporation was undercapitalized when it incurred its debts. *Francis*, 504 U.S. at xxx [or just 504 U.S. at xxx]. In fact, some state statutes have codified this principle. Del. Code Ann. tit. 42, §§ 119–xxx (19xx).

It is generally easier for a creditor to show that the corporation has been utilized as the shareholders' alter ego than to prove undercapitalization. Taylor, *supra*, §§ 142–148. As one Court has stated:

> The most common method of proving "alter ego" is to show either that the shareholders and the corporation have commingled their assets or that various corporate formalities have not been observed. Thus, the use of corporate funds by a shareholder to pay personal expenses may result in piercing of the veil. Similarly, failure of the corporation to observe basic corporate formalities such as holding meetings and elections may result in piercing of the veil.

Hays v. Anderson Adver. Co., 510 U.S. 10, xx (1997).

The majority shareholder of the Defendant in this case has acknowledged that the corporation held only one meeting in the past three years. (Hamilton Dep. at 14.) Similarly, the corporation has failed to hold any elections during that time period. "Elections of directors are an integral part of corporate existence. Failure to hold such elections *may well result* in 'piercing of the veil' such that shareholders are liable to corporate creditors." Susan B. Kimball & Jean B. Higgins, *Punitive Damages in Fraud Cases*, 18 Hous. L. Rev. 130, 146 (19xx). Other acts of neglect of the corporation can also be considered by courts in determining whether the corporate veil of limited liability can or should be pierced. *Hays*, 510 U.S. at xx [or just 510 U.S. at xx].

Because the evidence clearly establishes in this case that the Defendant corporation and Defendants Carol Yost and Joseph Yost have failed to observe even the most basic of corporate formalities, they should be denied the protection of corporate existence and be held liable for the corporation's obligations.

Pursuant to Fed. R. Civ. P. 53(a), Plaintiff thus urges this Court to grant his Motion to Strike Affirmative Defenses.

BRIEF 2

In the present case, the Plaintiff has argued that Defendant Anderson Herald Publishing Co. (hereinafter "Anderson") has abandoned its trademark through failure to use the mark. Defendant will show that such is not the case.

Trademarks are acquired through use. 15 U.S.C. § 1501 (19xx). Similarly, rights to trademarks can be lost through nonuse. 15 U.S.C. § 1554 (19xx). Abandonment of a trademark, however, is a serious loss and thus courts have typically refused to order that a mark has been abandoned unless there is clear and convincing evidence of such. *Hyatt v. Marshall Auto. Co.,* 12 F. Supp. 2d 101, xxx (D.D.C. 1995). In *Hyatt,* the court held that a press conference announcing that the company had selected a new mark to reflect its new corporate image and would cease use of the existing mark showed "a manifest intent to abandon the mark." *Id.* at xxx.

Other acts can also be used to support a finding of voluntary abandonment. For example, licensing the mark to another and failing to impose any requirements on the licensee's use of the mark is inconsistent with the owner's duty to monitor and protect its mark. Matthew J. Fletcher, III, Annotation, *Trademark Use and Policing,* 54 A.L.R.4th 118, xxx (1996). In fact, such an agreement is often called a "naked license" and may result in absolute loss of the mark to the licensee. *Id.* at 142–44. Once lost, such a mark cannot be reacquired. *Hyatt,* 12 F. Supp. 2d at xxx [or just 12 F. Supp. 2d at xxx].

Loss of trademark rights can also result from an extended period of nonuse. In fact, nonuse of a mark for three years creates a presumption that it has been abandoned. 15 U.S.C.A §§ 1059–1061 (West 19xx). Although the presumption is rebuttable, according to *Hyatt,* the evidence required to overcome the presumption must be compelling.

For example, it is possible that nonuse may be excusable. Courts have found that failure to use a mark because of transportation strikes preventing shipping, labor unrest, and acts of God may justify nonuse of a mark. Fletcher, *supra*, at 121. Nevertheless, failure to use a mark because of economic conditions rarely, if ever, justifies nonuse. *Nelson v. Constr. Distrib. Co.*, 989 F.2d 121, xxx (___ Cir. 1994), *aff'd*, 488 U.S. 16 (1995).

If an owner of a mark loses rights to the mark due to abandonment through nonuse and a third party begins using the mark, the owner cannot recreate rights in the mark through subsequent use. *Baker v. Carey*, 501 U.S. 116, xxx (1998); *Talbott Hous. Co. v. Mayfair Hills Inc.*, 901 F.2d 14, 16 (8th Cir.), *cert. denied*, 500 U.S. 28 (1998); 72 C.J.S. *Trademarks* § 72 (19xx). The original owner's rights, if any, stem from the date of its subsequent use. If such use is after that of the intervening third party, the third party has superior rights to the mark. *Nelson*, 989 F.2d at xxx [or just 989 F.2d at xxx].

Finally, a mere token use of a mark will not serve to defeat a presumption of nonuse. 3 J. Thomas McCarthy, *McCarthy on Trademarks and Unfair Competition* § 4.42 (4th ed. 1995). Thus, merely using the mark one time or using it in internal communications rather than for bona fide sales will not suffice. *Id.* § 4.47.

In the present case, Anderson's records show that use of the mark in question has been, at best, a token use. (Tracht Aff. ¶ 16.) Such use will not serve to overcome the presumption that Anderson's failure to use the mark for four years is an abandonment of the mark within the meaning of *Hyatt*, 12 F. Supp. 2d at xxx.

Thus, Plaintiff thus urges this Court to grant its Motion for Summary Judgment.

MEMORANDUM

To: Allen Amey
From: Susan Davis
Re: Claim of Sexual Harassment by Linda Denman
Date: September 30

Factual Background

Our client, Linda Denman ("Denman") is employed by Tech Solutions Integrators, Inc. ("TSI"). During the past six months, Denman, who is the only female on her project team, has noticed that the males on her team have engaged in sexually suggestive jokes and comments using crude language. Denman has been present during these conversations and has, on occasion, traded sexually suggestive quips with others on the team. Last week, one of the employees used his work desk computer to retrieve photographs of naked women from the Internet. The computer was placed so that any employee who walked by the desk could readily see the screen. Denman walked by, saw the photographs, and has inquired whether she may file a lawsuit against TSI alleging sexual harassment in the workplace.

Analysis

Section I: Introductory Principles. Sexual harassment is prosecuted as sexual discrimination under the Civil Rights Act of 1964. 42 U.S.C.S. §§ 2000e–xxxx (Law. Co-op. 19xx). While the language of the statute does not specifically address sexual harassment, case law has interpreted the statute to mean that sexual harassment is actionable as discrimination based on sex. Sara T. Garner, Annotation, *When the Workplace is Hostile,* 76 A.L.R. Fed. 158, 260–66 (19xx). The Supreme Court, in *Evans v. Merriman Guaranty Savings Bank,* 478 U.S. 67, xx (1987), citing federal employment regulation 29 C.F.R. § 1603.21(a) (19xx), found that two types of sexual harassment are actionable under the Act: harassment that conditions tangible employment benefits on sexual favors (referred to as *quid pro quo* harassment) and harassment that, while not affecting economic benefits, creates a hostile or offensive working environment ("hostile work environment" harassment). Because there is no evidence of *quid pro quo* harassment of Denman at TSI, any claim would be based on the hostile work environment at TSI.

The issue of Denman's participation in the conduct complained of will be discussed in Section II, *infra.*

In *Evans,* the Court relied on *Green v. EEOC,* 681 F.2d 897 (3d Cir. 1985), *aff'd,* 470 U.S. 904 (1986), for the standards required to find conduction actionable as "hostile work environment" harassment. The Court stated that the conduct must be so "severe or pervasive that it altered the conditions of . . . employment." 478 U.S. at 81.

The next year, the Court reiterated its decision in *Evans,* adding that to determine whether a hostile environment had been created the lower courts should consider all of the circumstances set forth in 29 C.F.R. § 1603.21 (19xx), such as the frequency of the conduct, whether the conduct was threatening or humiliating, and if the conduct interfered with the plaintiff's work performance. *Grayson v. Fording Sys. Inc.,* 509 U.S. 27, 33 (19xx).

Under these standards, sexual harassment need not be limited to unwanted physical contact, but can also include the display of obscene pictures. *Harrington v. Frederick Metro. Reprod. & Photo Co.*, 951 F. Supp. 403, 411 (C.D. Cal. 1996) (holding that photography company employee had a reasonable belief that an assignment to work on a sexually explicit photograph could constitute sexual harassment). However, in *Harding v. Harmony Foundation*, 13 F.3d 1004, xxxx (8th Cir.), *cert. denied*, 500 U.S. 16 (1996) [note: the reference to *cert. denied* may be omitted because the decision is more than two years old; the reference is included if the writer believes it is relevant], the court found that isolated incidents not directed specifically toward a plaintiff are merely offensive and not actionable as harassment. Relying upon *Foster v. FAA*, 776 F. Supp. 403 (E.D. Ark. 1992), the court in *Harding* stated that the conduct must be persistent to be actionable.

In *Grayson*, 509 U.S. at xx, the Supreme Court applied a two-pronged standard in determining whether conduct is actionable: an objective standard from a reasonable person's view and a subjective standard whether the claimant perceives the work environment to be abusive. Several state courts have stated that the objective standard is satisfied when the defendant creates an offensive environment and adversely affects the plaintiff's working conditions, as would be perceived by a reasonable person. *Fuller v. Bd. of Educ.*, 689 P.2d 91, xx (Cal. 1996). The defendant's conduct need not be intended as harassment and the adverse effect need not be pervasive. *Id.* Nor must the plaintiff prove a decline in tangible productivity. Garner, *supra* [or Garner, *supra*, at xxx].

Denman's case satisfies these standards. In *Otto v. Park Development Co.*, 699 P.2d 18, 21–26 (Cal. 1997), the court found that a single incident of leaving an adult magazine on the plaintiff's desk combined with gender-related harassment met the court's minimal *prima facie* standards of sexual harassment. Similarly, in the present case, if Denman's work environment was adversely affected due to the creation of a hostile working environment by TSI, the objective standard for proving sexual harassment has been satisfied.

APPENDIX Examples of State Cases and Statutes

Notes on cases: Some of the following examples are fictitious, and examples are not given for all cases from each state. Examples marked with footnotes 1 and 3 indicate the *Bluebook* form to be used when citing a state supreme court case or state appellate court case, respectively, in a document submitted to a state court in that state. Examples marked with footnotes 2 and 4 indicate the *Bluebook* form to be used when citing a state supreme court case or state appellate court case, respectively, in any other document, such as a legal memorandum or letter to a client. For states that no longer publish officially, the form shown is that now used in those states. For cases decided before the date on which those states ceased official publication, follow the format of cases shown in footnotes 1 and 3.

Notes on statutes: Although parentheticals are given following the statutes (showing date and publisher, if publication is not official), most practitioners omit the parenthetical information following statutes. Examples are not given for all statutory compilations for all states. A few examples are fictitious. Note that for many states, the *Bluebook* (Table T.1) indicates a preferred format for statutes, usually citation to the official set.

In all instances, court rules dictating citation form supersede the following forms.

Alabama*	*Employees' Benefit Ass'n v. Grissett,* 732 So. 2d 968, 972 (Ala. 1998).
	Davis v. State, 720 So. 2d 1006 (Ala. Crim. App. 1998).
	Alabama statute: Ala. Code § 37-2-83 (1992).
Alaska*	*Bostic v. State,* 968 P.2d 564, 566 (Alaska 1998).

	Linton v. State, 770 P.2d 123, 126 (Alaska Ct. App. 1994). Alaska statute: Alaska Stat. § 45.55.119 (Michie 1990).

Arizona	*In re Am. W. Airlines,* 179 Ariz. 528, 530, 880 P.2d 1075, 1777 (1998).[1] or
	   In re Am. W. Airlines, 880 P. 2d 1075, 1077 (Ariz. 1998).[2]
	Young v. Lee, 214 Ariz. App. 80, 84, 400 P.2d 103, 106 (1974).[3] or
	   Young v. Lee, 400 P.2d 103, 106 (Ariz. Ct. App. 1974).[4]
	State v. Wagner, 194 Ariz. 1, 4, 976 P.2d 250, 255 (Ct. App. 1998).[5]
	Allen v. Carr, 1999 Ariz. 12, ¶ 3, 901 P.2d 14.[8]
	Arizona statute: Ariz. Rev. Stat. Ann. § 28-7906 (West 1998).

Arkansas	*Powell v. Hays,* 323 Ark. 104, 106, 3 S.W.3d 15, 18 (1995).[1] or
	   Powell v. Hays, 3 S.W.3d 15, 18 (Ark. 1995).[2]
	Peters v. Boles, 56 Ark. App. 14, 19, 4 S.W.3d 90, 93 (1997).[3] or
	   Peters v. Boles, 4 S.W.3d 90, 93 (Ark. Ct. App. 1997).[4]
	Arkansas statute: Ark. Code Ann. § 5-64-401 (Michie 1996).

California	*People v. Ortega,* 19 Cal. 4th 686, 688, 968 P.2d 48, 50, 80 Cal. Rptr. 489, 491 (1998).[1] or
	   People v. Ortega, 968 P.2d 48, 50 (Cal. 1998).[2]
	Chu v. Lee, 33 Cal. App. 4th 80, 81, 229 Cal. Rptr. 6, 7 (1995).[3] or
	   Chu v. Lee, 229 Cal. Rptr. 6, 7 (Cal. Ct. App. 1995).
	California statute: Cal. Educ. Code § 8403 (West 1989).
	   Cal. Prob. Code § 1365 (Deering 1991).

Colorado*	*People v. Altman,* 960 P.2d 1164, 1168 (Colo. 1998). *Raney v. Feist,* 538 P.2d 89, 97 (Colo. Ct. App. 1990). *Harris v. Taylor,* 1998 Colo. 13, ¶ 8, 934 P.2d 18.[8] Colorado statute: Colo. Rev. Stat. § 31-10-408 (1999). Colo. Rev. Stat. Ann. § 14-10-119 (West 1997).

Connecticut	*State v. Cobb,* 251 Conn. 285, 288, 743 A.2d 1, 4 (1999).[1] or
	   State v. Cobb, 743 A.2d 1, 4 (Conn. 1999).[2]
	Easton v. Gibb, 245 Conn. App. 14, 19, 618 A.2d 49, 54 (1987).[3] or
	   Easton v. Gibb, 618 A.2d 49, 54 (Conn. App. Ct. 1987).[4]
	Connecticut statute: Conn. Gen. Stat. § 29-332 (1999).
	Conn. Gen. Stat. Ann. § 33-687 (West 1997).

Delaware*	*DiGiacobbe v. Sestak,* 743 A.2d 180, 185 (Del. 1999). *Rose v. Cadillac Fairview Shopping Ctr.,* 668 A.2d 782, 784 (Del. Super. Ct. 1995). Delaware statute: Del. Code Ann. tit. 13, § 733 (1989).
District of Columbia*	*Durham v. United States,* 743 A.2d 196, 199 (D.C. 1999). District of Columbia statute: D.C. Code Ann. § 6-972 (1995).
Florida*	*DiPietro v. Griefer,* 732 So. 2d 323, 326 (Fla. 1999). *Drury v. Jackson,* 438 So. 2d 568, 571 (Fla. Dist. Ct. App. 1987). Florida statute: Fla. Stat. ch. 421.04 (1993). Fla. Stat. Ann. § 443.036 (West 1997).

Georgia	*Allen v. Carr,* 216 Ga. 31, 37, 489 S.E.2d 15, 21 (1993).[1] or

Georgia

Allen v. Carr, 216 Ga. 31, 37, 489 S.E.2d 15, 21 (1993).[1] or
  Allen v. Carr, 489 S.E.2d 15, 21 (Ga. 1993).[2]
Clay v. Park, 177 Ga. App. 22, 26, 493 S.E.2d 57, 61 (1995).[3] or
  Clay v. Park, 493 S.E.2d 57, 61 (Ga. Ct. App. 1995).[4]
Georgia statute: Ga. Code Ann. § 49-4-149 (1998).
  Ga. Code Ann. § 38-2-93 (Harrison 1999).

Hawaii

State v. Maumalanga, 90 Haw. 58, 60, 976 P.2d 372, 375 (1998).[1] or
  State v. Maumalanga, 976 P.2d 372, 375 (Haw. 1998).[2]
Mann v. Kamalu, 89 Haw. App. 45, 47, 590 P.2d 18, 20 (1990).[3] or
  Mann v. Kamalu, 590 P.2d 18, 20 (Haw. Ct. App. 1990).[4]
State v. Perez, 90 Haw. 113, 115, 976 P.2d 427, 430 (Ct. App. 1998).[7] or
  State v. Perez, 976 P.2d 427, 430 (Haw. Ct. App. 1998).
Hawaii statute: Haw. Rev. Stat. § 516-32 (1997).
  Haw. Rev. Stat. Ann. § 516-62 (Michie 1993).

Idaho

West v. Sonke, 131 Idaho 133, 136, 968 P.2d 228, 231 (1998).[1] or
  West v. Sonke, 968 P.2d 228, 231 (Idaho 1998).[2]
State v. Pilik, 129 Idaho 50, 53, 921 P.2d 750, 754 (Ct. App. 1996).[3,5] or
  State v. Pilik, 921 P.2d 750, 754 (Idaho Ct. App. 1996).[4]
Idaho statute: Idaho Code § 56-805 (Michie 1994).

Illinois

LeGout v. Decker, 146 Ill. 2d 389, 391, 586
N.E.2d 1257, 1259, 166 Ill. Dec. 928, 931
(1992).[1] or
   LeGout v. Decker, 586 N.E.2d 1257, 1259
   (Ill. 1992).[2]
Martinez v. Mobil Oil Corp., 296 Ill. App. 3d
607, 610, 694 N.E.2d 639, 641, 230 Ill. Dec. 670,
674 (1998).[3] or
   Martinez v. Mobil Oil Corp., 694 N.E.2d
   639, 641 (Ill. App. Ct. 1998).[4]
Illinois statute: 735 Ill. Comp. Stat. 5/1-104
                    (1993).
                    405 Ill. Comp. Stat. Ann. 5/2-
                    107.1 (West 1997).

Indiana*

In re Edwards, 694 N.E.2d 701, 704 (Ind. 1998).
Knaus v. York, 586 N.E.2d 909, 914 (Ind. Ct.
App. 1992).
Indiana statute: Ind. Code § 28-5-1-9 (1998).
                   Ind. Code Ann. § 6-1.1-17-3
                   (Michie 1998).
                   Ind. Code Ann. § 28-2-16-17
                   (West 1996).

Iowa*

In re Wagner, 604 N.W.2d 605, 607 (Iowa 2000).
State v. Hauan, 361 N.W.2d 336, 336 (Iowa Ct.
App. 1984).
Iowa statute: Iowa Code § 422.86 (1999).
                Iowa Code Ann. § 524.106
                (West 1993).

Kansas

State v. Valentine, 260 Kan. 431, 433, 921 P.2d
770, 773 (1996).[1] or
   State v. Valentine, 921 P.2d 770, 773 (Kan.
   1996).[2]
Bryson v. Wichita State Univ., 19 Kan. App. 2d
1104, 1107, 880 P.2d 800, 804 (1994).[3] or
   Bryson v. Wichita State Univ., 880 P.2d 800,
   804 (Kan. Ct. App. 1994).[4]
Kansas statute: Kan. Stat. Ann. § 24-621
                  (1993).

Kan. U.C.C. Ann. § 84-2-604
(West 1996).

Kentucky*

Harrington v. Phifer, 4 S.W.3d 918, 929 (Ky.
1995).
O'Malley v. Gonzales, 6 S.W.3d 404, 418 (Ky. Ct.
App. 1998).
Kentucky statute: Ky. Rev. Stat. Ann.
§ 199.470 (Banks-Baldwin
1994).
Ky. Rev. Stat. Ann.
§ 186.412 (Michie 1997).

Louisiana*

Neely v. Turner, 720 So. 2d 673, 675 (La. 1992).
Medicus v. Scott, 744 So. 2d 192, 195 (La. Ct.
App. 1993).
Smith v. Jones, 94-2345, p. 7 (La. 7/15/94); 650
So.2d 500, 504.
Louisiana statute: La. Rev. Stat. Ann.
§ 23:1142 (West 1998).
La. Code Crim. Proc. Ann.
art. 786 (West 1998).[8]

Maine*, +

D'Souza v. Garner, 690 A.2d 671, 685 (Me.
1995).
Smith v. Jones, 1997 ME 7, ¶ 14, 685 A.2d 110,
112.[8]
Maine statute: Me. Rev. Stat. Ann. tit. 25,
§ 2921 (West 1998).

Maryland

Save Our Streets v. Mitchell, 357 Md. 237, 239,
743 A.2d 748, 750 (1998).[1] or
Save Our Streets v. Mitchell, 743 A.2d 748,
750 (Md. 1998).[2]
Allied Inv. Corp. v. Jasen, 123 Md. App. 88, 90,
716 A.2d 1085, 1088 (1998).[3] or
Allied Inv. Corp. v. Jasen, 716 A.2d 1085,
1088 (Md. Ct. Spec. App. 1998).[4]
Maryland statute: Md. Code Ann., Fam. Law
§ 7-101 (1999).

Massachusetts

In re London, 427 Mass. 477, 479, 694 N.E.2d
337, 339 (1998).[1] or

In re London, 694 N.E.2d 337, 339 (Mass. 1998).[2]

Campbell v. City Council of Lynn, 32 Mass. App. Ct. 152, 155, 586 N.E.2d 1009, 1013 (1992).[3] or

Campbell v. City Council of Lynn, 586 N.E.2d 1009, 1013 (Mass. App. Ct. 1992).[4]

Massachusetts statute: Mass. Gen. Laws Ann. ch. 175, § 123 (West 1988).

Mass. Ann. Laws ch. 183, § 30 (Law. Co-op. 1996).

Michigan	*Maynard v. Sauseda,* 417 Mich. 1100, 1103, 361 N.W.2d 342, 345 (1983).[1] or

Maynard v. Sauseda, 361 N.W.2d 342, 345 (Mich. 1983).[2]

Bass v. Combs, 238 Mich. App. 16, 19, 604 N.W.2d 727, 730 (1999).[3] or

Bass v. Combs, 604 N.W.2d 727, 730 (Mich. Ct. App. 1999).[4]

Michigan statute: Mich Comp. Laws § 120.904 (1996).

Mich. Comp. Laws Ann. § 380.1756 (West 1997).

Minnesota*

Knotz v. Viking Carpet, 361 N.W.2d 872, 877 (Minn. 1985).

Boldt v. Roth, 604 N.W.2d 117, 120 (Minn. Ct. App. 2000).

Minnesota statute: Minn. Stat. § 50.28 (1998).

Minn. Stat. Ann. § 541.04 (West 1988).

Mississippi*

Lindsay v. State, 720 So. 2d 182, 185 (Miss. 1996).

Ladner v. Manuel, 744 So. 2d 390, 394 (Miss. Ct. App. 1997).

Smith v. Jones, 95–KA–01234–SCT (¶1) (Miss. 1998).[8] or

Smith v. Jones, 699 So. 2d 100 (¶1) (Miss. 1998).
Mississippi statute: Miss. Code Ann. § 65-11-45 (1996).

Missouri*

Lovell v. B & H Inc., 909 S.W.2d 14, 18 (Mo. 1993).
Bryson v. Brant, 925 S.W.2d 689, 694 (Mo. Ct. App. 1995).
Missouri statute: Mo. Rev. Stat. § 367.040 (1994).
Mo. Ann. Stat. § 534.030 (West 1988).

Montana⁺

Horn v. Horn, 165 Mont. 118, 129, 921 P.2d 14, 23 (1996).[1] or
Horn v. Horn, 921 P.2d 14, 23 (Mont. 1996).[2]
Dawson v. Walter, 1998 MT 12, ¶44, 286 Mont. 175, ¶44, 968 P.2d 1312, ¶44.[8]
Montana statute: Mont. Code Ann. § 69-1-224 (1995).

Nebraska

State v. Nebraska, 258 Neb. 511, 513, 604 N.W.2d 151, 154 (2000).[1] or
State v. Nebraska, 604 N.W.2d 151, 154 (Neb. 2000).[2]
Reinsch v. Reinsch, 8 Neb. Ct. App. 852, 854, 602 N.W.2d 261, 264 (1999).[3] or
Reinsch v. Reinsch, 602 N.W.2d 261, 264 (Neb. Ct. App. 1999).[4]
Nebraska statute: Neb. Rev. Stat. § 72–221 (1996).
Neb. Rev. Stat. Ann. § 54-101 (Michie 1995).

Nevada⁺

Shaw v. Gammon, 113 Nev. 24, 29, 960 P.2d 18, 23 (1998).[1] or
Shaw v. Gammon, 960 P.2d 18, 23 (Nev. 1998).[2]
Nevada statute: Nev. Rev. Stat. § 243.490 (1999).

Nev. Rev. Stat. Ann.
§ 319.350 (Lexis 1999).[6]

New Hampshire[+]

Moore v. Tyler, 89 N.H. 114, 118, 743 A.2d 681,
686 (1999).[1] or
Moore v. Tyler, 743 A.2d 681, 686 (N.H.
1999).[2]
New Hampshire statute: N.H. Rev. Stat. Ann.
§ 391:7 (Lexis
1998).[6]

New Jersey

Roach v. TRW, Inc., 162 N.J. 195, 197, 743 A.2d
847, 850 (1999).[1] or
Roach v. TRW, Inc., 743 A.2d 847, 850 (N.J.
1999).[2]
Bell v. Bell, 312 N.J. Super. 13, 15, 716 A.2d 318,
321 (1998).[3] or
Bell v. Bell, 716 A.2d 318, 321 (N.J. Super.
Ct. App. Div. 1998).[4]
New Jersey statute: N.J. Stat. Ann. § 17:48-6
(West 1996).

New Mexico

Barone v. Torres, 127 N.M. 20, 23, 976 P.2d 21,
24 (1994).[1] or
Barone v. Torres, 976 P.2d 21, 24 (N.M.
1994).[2]
State v. Ray, 1998-NMSC-001, ¶ 4, 122 N.M. 23,
26.[8]
State v. Ray, 1998-NMSC-001, ¶ 4, 976 P.2d 54,
56.[8]
Key v. Chrysler Motors Corp., 127 N.M. 98, 99,
976 P.2d 523, 524 (Ct. App. 1994).[3,5] or
Key v. Chrysler Motors Corp., 976 P.2d 523,
524 (N.M. Ct. App. 1994).[4]
New Mexico statute: N.M. Stat. Ann. § 31-2-
3 (Michie 1997).
NMSA 1978, § 31-2-3
(1996).[8]

New York

Furch v. Bacci, 91 N.Y.2d 953, 955, 694 N.E.2d
880, 882, 666 N.Y.S.2d 300, 302 (1998).[1] or

Furch v. Bacci, 694 N.E.2d 880, 882 (N.Y. 1998).[2]

Pryce v. Fowell, 257 A.D.2d 275, 277, 594 N.Y.S.2d 82, 84 (1997).[3] or

Pryce v. Fowell, 594 N.Y.S.2d 82, 84 (App. Div. 1997).[4]

Macy v. Frye, 108 Misc. 2d 994, 997, 438 N.Y.S.2d 156, 160 (Sup. Ct. 1980).[3] or

Macy v. Frye, 438 N.Y.S.2d 156, 160 (Sup. Ct. 1980).[4]

New York statute: N.Y. Dom. Rel. Law § 23 (McKinney 1999).

N.Y. Gen. Bus. Law § 353 (Lexis 1999).[6]

North Carolina

O'Brien v. Matthews, 280 N.C. 42, 47, 185 S.E.2d 123, 126 (1975).[1] or

O'Brien v. Matthews, 185 S.E.2d 123, 126 (N.C. 1975).[2]

Mill v. Lodge, 5 N.C. App. 657, 659, 169 S.E.2d 36, 39 (1969).[3] or

Mill v. Lodge, 169 S.E.2d 36, 39 (N.C. Ct. App. 1969).[4]

North Carolina statute: N.C. Gen. Stat. § 34-2 (1999).

N.C. Gen. Stat. Ann. § 105-33 (Lexis 1999).[6]

North Dakota*

Lyon v. Ford Motor Co., 604 N.W.2d 453, 455 (N.D. 1996).

Fabricut, Inc. v. Keeney, 429 N.W.2d 24, 29 (N.D. Ct. App. 1988).

Adams v. North, 1999 ND 32, ¶4, 600 NW2d 91.[8]

North Dakota statute: N.D. Cent. Code § 30.1-35-01 (1996).

Ohio

Columbus Bar Ass'n v. Dye, 82 Ohio St. 3d 64, 67, 694 N.E.2d 440, 443 (1998).[1] or

Columbus Bar Ass'n v. Dye, 694 N.E.2d 440, 443 (Ohio 1998).[2]

Brown v. Dana, 66 Ohio App. 3d 709, 711, 586
N.E.2d 150, 153 (1990).[3] or
> *Brown v. Dana,* 586 N.E.2d 150, 153 (Ohio
> Ct. App. 1990).[4]

Ohio statute: Ohio Rev. Code Ann. § 4507.3
(Anderson 1999).
Ohio Rev. Code Ann. § 101.5
(West 1999).

Oklahoma*

Nation v. State Farm Ins. Co., 880 P.2d 877, 890
(Okla. 1994).
Peterson v. Baker, 921 P.2d 955, 963 (Okla. Ct.
App. 1996).
Skelly v. State, 880 P.2d 401, 405 (Okla. Crim.
App. 1994).
Gray v. Carey, 1999 OK 44, ¶4, 978 P.2d 490.[8]

Oklahoma statute: Okla. Stat. tit. 73, § 83.2
(1991).
Okla. Stat. Ann. tit. 68,
§ 1353 (West 1992).

Oregon

Tellam v. Birch, 321 Or. 1, 3, 921 P.2d 380, 384
(1996).[1] or
> *Tellam v. Birch,* 921 P.2d 380, 384 (Or.
> 1996).[2]

Enders v. Enders, 154 Or. App. 142, 144, 960
P.2d 986, 989 (1997).[3] or
> *Enders v. Enders,* 960 P.2d 986, 989 (Or. Ct.
> App. 1997).[4]

Oregon statute: Or. Rev. Stat. § 576.175
(1997).
Or. Rev. Stat. Ann.
§ 657A.290 (Butterworth
Supp. 1994).

Pennsylvania

Cope v. Miller, 389 Pa. 116, 119, 716 A.2d 18, 22
(1998).[1] or
> *Cope v. Miller,* 716 A.2d 18, 22 (Pa. 1998).[2]

Hardy v. Sells, 422 Pa. Super. 4, 9, 639 A.2d 909,
914 (1993).[3] or
> *Hardy v. Sells,* 639 A.2d 909, 914 (Pa.
> Super. Ct. 1993).[4]

	Pennsylvania statute:	23 Pa. Cons. Stat. § 5303 (1997). Pa. Stat. Ann. tit. 63, § 224 (West 1996).

Rhode Island*,+

Estrada v. Walker, 743 A.2d 1026, 1034 (R.I. 1999).

Rhode Island statute: R.I. Gen. Laws § 42-64-9 (1998).

South Carolina

Sullivan v. Pine, 331 S.C. 190, 199, 502 S.E.2d 19, 29 (1998).[1] or
> *Sullivan v. Pine,* 502 S.E.2d 19, 29 (S.C. 1998).[2]

McKee v. Hall, 331 S.C. 560, 566, 500 S.E.2d 909, 914 (Ct. App. 1993).[3,5] or
> *McKee v. Hall,* 500 S.E.2d 909, 914 (S.C. Ct. App. 1993).[4]

South Carolina statute: S.C. Code Ann. § 44-7-220 (Law. Co-op. 1985).

South Dakota*,+

Meinders v. Weber, 604 N.W.2d 148, 150 (S.D. 1995).

Hoogestraat v. Barnett, 1998 SD 104, ¶5, 595 NW2d 900.[8]

South Dakota statute: S.D. Codified Laws § 29A-2-21 (Michie 1997).

Tennessee*

Booker v. Allen, 931 S.W.2d 970, 977 (Tenn. 1993).

Davis v. Crane, 918 S.W.2d 887, 892 (Tenn. Ct. App. 1987).

State v. Doyle, 920 S.W.2d 101, 104 (Tenn. Crim. App. 1989).

Tennessee statute: Tenn. Code Ann. § 17-1-304 (1994).

Texas*

Kroger Co. v. Robins, 5 S.W.3d 221, 224 (Tex. 1999).

Peterson v. Reyna, 920 S.W.2d 285, 288 (Tex. Crim. App. 1994).

Texas statute: Tex. Educ. Code Ann. § 102.12
(Vernon 1991).

Utah*   *Salt Lake City v. Smoot,* 921 P.2d 1003, 1005
(Utah 1996).
Gregory v. Hendrix, 880 P.2d 18, 24 (Utah Ct.
App. 1994).
Allen v. Ray, 1999 UT 240, ¶4, 16 P.3d 1, 7.
Utah statute: Utah Code Ann. § 39-6-37
(1998).

Vermont⁺   *Winn v. Riley,* 161 Vt. 16, 24, 743 A.2d 209, 214
(1999).[1] or
   Winn v. Riley, 743 A.2d 209, 214 (Vt.
   1994).[2]
Vermont statute: Vt. Stat. Ann. tit. 24, § 1312
(1992).

Virginia   *Sheldon v. Drye,* 225 Va. 11, 19, 445 S.E.2d 89,
94 (1995).[1] or
   Sheldon v. Drye, 445 S.E.2d 89, 94 (Va.
   1995).[2]
Ruiz v. Harley, 25 Va. App. 16, 20, 486 S.E.2d
90, 95 (1997).[3] or
   Ruiz v. Harley, 486 S.E.2d 90, 95 (Va. Ct.
   App. 1997).[4]
Virginia statute: Va. Code Ann. § 33.1-226
(Michie 1996).

Washington   *Brewer v. Brewer,* 137 Wash. 2d 756, 758, 976
P.2d 102, 104 (1999).[1] or
   Brewer v. Brewer, 976 P.2d 102, 104 (Wash.
   1999).[2]
State v. Hunt, 75 Wash. App. 795, 797, 880 P.2d
96, 99 (1994).[3] or
   State v. Hunt, 880 P.2d 96, 99 (Wash. Ct.
   App. 1994).[4]
Washington statute: Wash. Rev. Code
§ 80.36.310 (1998).
Wash. Rev. Code Ann.
§ 35.21.403 (West 1990).

West Virginia[+]   *Farrel v. Bond,* 156 W. Va. 450, 456, 295 S.E.2d
                                19, 25 (1973).[1] or
                                      Farrel v. Bond, 295 S.E.2d 19, 25 (W. Va.
                                      1973).[2]
                                West Virginia statute: W. Va. Code § 17A-4-5
                                                         (1996).
                                                         W. Va. Code Ann. § 19-
                                                         104 (Michie 19xx).

Wisconsin   *In re Parsons,* 122 Wis. 2d 186, 188, 361 N.W.2d
                                687, 690 (1985).[1] or
                                      In re Parsons, 361 N.W.2d 687, 690 (Wis.
                                      1985).[2]
                                Smith v. Jones, 2000 WI 14, ¶6.[8] or
                                      Smith v. Jones, 214 Wis. 2d 408, ¶12.
                                State v. Schultz, 145 Wis. 2d 661, 663, 429
                                N.W.2d 79, 81 (Ct. App. 1988).[3,5] or
                                      State v. Schultz, 429 N.W.2d 79, 81 (Wis.
                                      Ct. App. 1988).[4]
                                Doe v. Roe, 2000 WI App 9, ¶17.[8] or
                                      Doe v. Roe, 595 N.W.2d 346, ¶27.
                                Wisconsin statute: Wis. Stat. § 480.08 (1996).
                                                     Wis. Stat. Ann. § 70.22
                                                     (West 1999).

Wyoming[*,+]   *Ruwart v. Wagner,* 880 P.2d 586, 590 (Wyo.
                                1994).
                                Wyoming statute: Wyo. Stat. Ann. § 39-16-
                                                   210 (Lexis 1999).[6]

---

*State no longer publishes officially.

⁺State has no intermediate appellate courts.

[1]Case from supreme court of the state being cited in a document submitted to state court in that state.

[2]Case from state supreme court being cited in a document other than court document, such as a legal memorandum or letter to client.

[3]Case from state intermediate court being cited in a document submitted to state court in that state.

[4]Case from state intermediate court being cited in a document other than court document, such as a legal memorandum or letter to client.

[5]Appellate court cases are published in same volumes as supreme court cases; thus, parenthetical information is needed to identify the court that decided the case.

[6]Lexis Law Publishing has begun publishing a number of unofficial state statutes.

[7]Beginning in 1994, Hawaii appellate court cases are also published in *Hawaii Reports.*

[8]Vendor neutral or public domain citation form.

Index

A

ABA Legal Technology Resource Center, Uniform Citation Standards, 61
Abbreviations in case names, 13–14
Administrative decisions, 52–54
Administrative materials:
    administrative decisions, 52–54
    agency law, 51
    presidential and executive materials, 54
    rules and regulations, 51–52
    Treasury regulations, 52
Agency law, 51
Alabama, 18
A.L.R. annotations, 48–49
Alterations, 71–72
American Association of Law Libraries (AALL), 19, 59
American Bar Association (ABA), 19, 59–60
American Jurisprudence, 47
American Law Reports, 48
Arizona, 18, 21, 61
Arkansas, 21, 61
Asking for help, 4–5
At, use of, 78

B

Bills, 38–39
Bluebook, 1–2
    administrative materials
        Rule 14, 51–54
    A.L.R. annotations
        Rule 16.6.5, 48–49
    alterations
        Rule 5.2, 71–72
    books and treatises
        Rule 15, 45–46
    capitalization
        Rule 8; P.6, 85–86
    case names
        abbreviations in, 13–14
        Rule 10.2, 11–14
    constitutions
        Rule 11, 41
    court rules
        Rule 12.8.3, 41
    dictionaries
        Rule 15.7, 47
    encyclopedias
        Rule 15.7, 47–48
    federal court cases
        Table T.1, 25–28
    history of, 3
    internal cross-references
        Rule 3.6, 92–93